The Geologist of the Soul

The Geologist of the Soul

Talks on Rebbe-craft and Spiritual Leadership

Rabbi Zalman Schachter-Shalomi

With contributions by
Netanel Miles-Yépez

Edited by
N.M-Y.

Albion
Andalus
Boulder, Colorado
2012

*"The old shall be renewed,
and the new shall be made holy."*

— Rabbi Avraham Yitzhak Kook

Copyright © 2012 Zalman M. Schachter-Shalomi

First edition with corrections. All rights reserved.

No part of this book may be reproduced or transmitted in any form or by any means, electronic or mechanical, including photocopy, recording, or any information storage or retrieval system, except for brief passages in connection with a critical review, without permission in writing from the publisher:

Albion-Andalus Inc.
P. O. Box 19852
Boulder, CO 80308
www.albionandalus.com

Design and composition by Albion-Andalus Inc.

Cover design by Daryl McCool, D.A.M. Cool Graphics.

Cover artwork: "Last Prayer" by Samuel Hirschenberg.

Manufactured in the United States of America

ISBN-13: 978-0615748467 (Albion-Andalus Books)

ISBN-10: 0615748465

To my Rebbes and Mentors

Contents

Acknowledgments

Preface   xi

First Talk: *Rebbe Training 101*   1
Second Talk: *The Soul-Cluster of the Rebbe*   23
Third Talk: *The Rebbe and Spiritual Typologies*   41
Fourth Talk: *The Rebbe's Assessment of the Hasid's Spiritual Situation*   59
Fifth Talk: *The Rebbe's Compassion and Prayer-work*   83
Sixth Talk: *The Rebbe's Tool-box for Intercession*   97
Seventh Talk: *A Dialogue on the Vocation of Being a Rebbe*   117

Appendix: *Training the Rebbes of the Future*   131
Geologists of the Soul Forum

Acknowledgments

I WISH TO THANK Netanel Miles-Yépez for editing this collection into its present form. Most of the material came from a series of talks given at Elat Chayyim Jewish Retreat Center in 1996. These talks were then supplemented by other short talks given to my student, Rabbi Ruth Gan Kagan's class on intercessory prayer in 2006, and by a dialogue with my student, Reb Netanel Miles-Yépez, on the subject of the book in 2012. I am also indebted to my secretary, Mary Fulton for all her work on the transcripts, and to Leigh Ann Dillinger who took careful notes from my talks in Reb Ruth's class and who also, with my friend Tessa Bielecki, proofread the manuscript.

— Z.M.S-S.

Preface

ONCE, WHEN I WAS STILL a Hillel director at the University of Manitoba in Winnipeg, I took a group of my students to meet my Rebbe, Rabbi Menachem Mendel Schneerson (1902-1994), the seventh Rebbe of Lubavitcher Rebbe. At that time, I served as the translator for them, translating into English from the Rebbe's Yiddish.

When the students got the opportunity to ask questions, one of them boldly asked the Rebbe, "What's a Rebbe good for?" I could have sunk through the floor in embarrassment; but the Rebbe wasn't offended at all and gave this wonderful answer:

"I can't speak about myself; but I can tell you about my own Rebbe. For me, my Rebbe was the geologist of the soul. You see, there are so many treasures in the earth. There is gold, there is silver, and there are diamonds. But if you don't know where to dig, you'll only find dirt and rocks and mud. The Rebbe can tell you where to dig, and what to dig for, but the digging you must do yourself."[1]

More than any other spiritual analogy I know, this *mashal* from my Rebbe best puts the role of Rebbe into its proper context, emphasizing the Rebbe's function over identity, and not taking the responsibility for doing the spiritual work away from the disciple. Thus, I have drawn the title for this series of edited talks from it and would ask you to keep it continually in mind as you read.

— *Rabbi Zalman Schachter-Shalomi*
Boulder, Colorado, 2012

---

[1] More of this conversation is included in Lawrence Kirschenbaum, *The Rebbe: Inspiring a Generation* (2008).

First Talk

Rebbe Training 101

I'LL BEGIN WITH SOME THEORY, but will soon follow with what I hope will be the beginning of a process.

Although you try to be as honest as you can when writing a course description, the description is often deceiving. After all, how can I truly say that this is going to be "Rebbe Training 101"? I can imagine a Hasid in Brooklyn laughing and saying: "*Oy! Gevalt!* You're gonna' talk to these *am ha'aratzim*, these 'ignorant folks,' who aren't even *shomer Shabbat*, who don't 'keep the Sabbath,' and probably don't even know an *aveira* from a *mitzvah*, about becoming Rebbes? A Rebbe is a *tzaddik*, a 'righteous person,' someone we call *adoneinu moreinu v'rabbeinu*, 'our lord, teacher and master,' a *butzina kaddisha*, a 'holy candle.' And you're going to take people off the street and talk to them about becoming Rebbes?! They have to become *real Jews* first. Then, *maybe*, they can aspire to become Hasidim! But Rebbes? Foolishness."

I remember how my mentor, Professor Abraham Joshua Heschel once said to me, "Reb Zalman—*zugt nisht altz-ding oys*—you don't have to tell them everything." As if to say, not everything is to be told or taught; we have to keep some things back. When I heard this, I understood what he was saying, and could appreciate where he was coming from. And yet, at the same time, this emerging paradigm demands more of what was held back in the past.

None of you could be where you are now if you hadn't struggled, if you hadn't done some God-wrestling, if you hadn't in some way responded to a call. And in answering that call, you accept that you are being *deployed* and sent on a journey. To what end? To be Hasidic Rebbes? No, that's not what I am saying here.

There is a wonderful story about a man who came to the Kotzker Rebbe, Reb Menachem Mendel of Kotzk, and said to him, "Rebbe, my father came to me in a dream and told me I should be a Rebbe." The Kotzker Rebbe laughed and said, "If your father had come to 300 people and told them you were to be their Rebbe, that I would take more seriously. That *you* had a dream to be a Rebbe is not so significant."

And with that, he puts the matter into the proper perspective. Is a Rebbe such a common thing that you can simply take a course and become a Rebbe? Of course not—a Rebbe is an exemplary model of spiritual leadership. But, as such, there is something we can learn from the Rebbe's example. And this is what we are talking about here.

The Rebbe as Tzaddik

When Reb Shneur Zalman of Liadi described the *tzaddik gamur*, the 'completely righteous person,' as one without a shred of *yetzer ha'ra*, or 'evil inclination,' he had effectively priced the complete *tzaddik* out of the market for us. *Ki horgo be'ta'anit*, 'with great austerity,' the *tzaddik gamur* had killed the *yetzer ha'ra* within. Who can even come close to this kind of accomplishment today?

Thank God, the same Reb Shneur Zalman wrote a book called *Sefer Shel Beinonim*, the 'book of the people in-between,' which makes up the first section of his *Tanya*. In it, he makes a very important statement from the point of view of behavior. If the *beinoni*, the 'in-betweener,' and the *tzaddik*, the 'righteous person' are praying in the same *shul* together, you can't tell the difference between them on the outside. That is because, on the level of behavior, the *beinoni* and the *tzaddik* are the same (according to Reb Shneur Zalman's definition). But internally, while the *tzaddik* is totally good and no longer tempted by evil, the *beinoni* only just manages to control his *mahshava, dibbur* and *ma'aseh*, 'thought, word and deed.' The *beinoni* only manages to do this with great effort and struggle, because the *beinoni* doesn't want to slip even for one moment and become an instrument of the energy system of evil, or *k'lippah*.

When asked what he was, Reb Shneur Zalman quoted Rav, saying, *K'gon ana beinoni*, "I'm a *beinoni*." The interesting thing is that in the Talmud, they say to Rav, "If you are a *beinoni—lo shovik mahayah l'khol b'riyah*—you don't leave any room for any of us to be anything other than evil!" We are, at best, according to the *Tanya*, *r'sha'im sh'einam g'murim*, not all together wicked. That is the best that can be said of us! Even in behavior, we are very far from being in the halakhic 'black.' If that's the case, then the question arises again—What right have we to aspire to 'Rebbe-hood?'

Let's let this question dangle for a moment and we'll come back to it again later.

In 1994, shortly after the passing of Rabbi Menachem Mendel Schneerson, the seventh Lubavitcher Rebbe, and my friend, Rabbi Shlomo Carlebach, I looked around at the Jewish world and saw that there were very few of the 'old guard' left. The Gerer Rebbe had recently passed on, the Bobover Rebbe was ailing, and I felt like I was witnessing a *Götterdämmerung*, a 'twilight of the gods' in Hasidism.

When I first encountered Habad Hasidism, what attracted me was its contemplative focus on *hitbon'nut,* meditation or contemplation, and *davvenen b'arikhut,* 'taking your time in prayer,' praying contemplatively. To do these practices, you had to deepen your knowing and have a great deal of understanding which you could apply *ada'ata d'nafshei,* thinking in the context of your own situation. Then, thinking deeply in this way, the appropriate affect follows naturally.

In those years, I saw in Habad Hasidism a contemplative approach to Hasidism that I didn't see in other Hasidic lineages. Elsewhere, I saw good people studying Talmud, being extremely careful about *mitzvot,* and even *davvenen,* or 'praying' with great fervor. But the fervor was something that seemed like flaming wood, burning and smoking on the outside; it didn't always seem to have that blue flame of very strong heat that came from a contemplative focus. I loved it when I first heard that Reb Shneur Zalman had cried out in his *davvenen*—"I don't want your World-to-Come! I don't want enlightenment! I only want You alone!" That kind of powerful yearning and longing excited me.

When my Rebbe, Reb Yosef Yitzhak Schneersohn, the sixth Lubavitcher Rebbe—who at that point was partially paralyzed—would tell us a story, with all the difficulty he had in expressing himself through the paralysis, he never got lazy and omitted an adjective in his description of the scene. In this way, he allowed us to develop the 'imaginative faculty,' the *hush ha'tziyur.* In other words, he told stories in such a way that he placed us *inside* that scene. And when he was teaching, I had the sense that he was showing me a horizon that I would not have seen ordinarily.

Later, it seemed to me, that Habad Hasidism turned from its contemplative focus to the apostolic work of Mitzvah Tanks.

First Talk: Rebbe Training 101

I'm not criticizing it—it was needed. I'm just sad that the Yeshiva University folks didn't make their own Mitzvah Tanks, going out to teach Jews on the street how to do those *mitzvot,* leaving Habad Hasidim free to pursue in their contemplative work in *hokhmah, binah* and *da'at* (HaBaD—'wisdom, understanding, and knowledge').

As my late *mashpiyya,* Rabbi Yisroel Jacobson, put it, "They left the inner *mahaneh kehunah* for the outer *mahaneh Yisrael.*" That is to say, the inner work of the priestly camp was abandoned for the common outer work of Israel.

During the years I knew the late Lubavitcher Rebbe, Rabbi Menachem Mendel Schneerson, I saw two people in him. One of them said that he was *not* the Rebbe, but merely the previous Rebbe's *shaliah,* or 'emissary,' modeling the *shaliah* role and holding his father-in-law's vision. But the other was clearly a Rebbe who, paradoxically, was turning the charismatic Rebbe situation into an institution—the Habad House. When the institution was firmly in place, and the bookcases of the library were full of his teachings, he felt he could pass on in peace. He was concerned that even simple people should have some kind of contact with him through his teachings and institutions, which would remain active and in force long after he was gone.

In a stroke of genius, he started giving out dollar bills, making people emissaries of his charity. It was an amazing thing for them to receive a dollar bill from him. Why "genius"? I also saw people come to the Hindu *guru,* Baba Muktananda, years ago, desiring a *mantra* from him. He would reach into a box and hand it to the person, and you just knew that little slip of paper would be treasured for a lifetime. Likewise, you would see people standing outside of '770'—Lubavitch Headquarters on 770 Eastern Parkway—looking admiringly at the dollar bill they had just gotten from the Rebbe. They weren't about to let that dollar go! There was even a guy outside '770' who sold pictures of the Rebbe that he would laminate onto the dollar bills in place of George Washington!

You see, that dollar was precious to the people who had received it from the Rebbe's hand. Imagine opening your wallet and catching sight of the Rebbe's special dollar bill in there, neatly folded! What are you going to do with your other money after you've seen that? So the Rebbe's dollar bill is already doing what a *mezuzah* and *tzitzit* and *t'fillin* are supposed to do—to be reminders, keeping you on the path!

So it was genius; but, at the same time, I regret that he did not spend his last years developing a cadre of new Rebbes.

A Low Threshold

Rabbi Shlomo Carlebach and I got into our situation, and all that has happened since, because our Rebbe, Rabbi Yosef Yitzhak Schneersohn, called us to his table on *Yud-Tet-Kislev* in 1949 and said, "It's time that you should travel to the campuses, to the universities." And we agreed that we would go as just plain "Zalman and Shlomo," keeping the threshold for how we would present ourselves very low. It was not necessarily helpful to be "Rabbi Carlebach and Rabbi Schachter," because we wanted to meet people where they were, without the barriers those titles might create. And I think it was successful because many people felt, "I can do that too!" We were just telling stories and singing songs and talking about what we loved. So stepping into our shoes became relatively easy.

Once, when I was *davvenen* at the *Kotel*, the remains of the Western Wall in Jerusalem, for guidance about the Rebbe role into which I had been thrust, I got the message that I should go see the Bobover Rebbe. So I went to see him and wrote my question about functioning as a Rebbe on a *kvittel*—the small slip of paper on which you make a request of a Rebbe—and he answered me, saying: "You are going to have a hard time doing *t'shuvah,* 'repenting.' It is one thing if someone does something wrong in behavior, realizes the error, and then goes back to the straight-and-narrow. But you have changed the boundary-lines, so that you are not going to go back to the old *Yiddishkeit,* to the previous paradigm of Judaism. Your *aveiras*, the places where you are getting off-track, are in *hokhmah, binah* and *da'at*—the three spheres of divine intellection. You think of new paradigms; therefore, you are not going to be able to do *t'shuvah* easily and come back to the traditionally defined straight-and-narrow." And he was right.

But you can't push the baby back into the womb after it's been born. What I wanted from him were some of the teachings he may have gotten from his father on how to read a *kvittel,* or prayer-request; how to do what a Rebbe does when a Hasid comes with a request, reading from the *kvittel* as if reading from the 'Akashic record' of the Hasid. But the Bobover Rebbe didn't answer me in any direct way. Nevertheless, I felt the need was urgent. After all, who was going to do the 'hidden work' of discernment for people outside of the traditional fold, responding to their souls and giving them genuine spiritual direction for transformation from the deepest sources. And this feeling has only gotten stronger having witnessed the *Götterdämmerung* happening all around me in Hasidism.

So who was going to do that work? It is easy to learn how to do a *tish,* a Hasidic gathering around the *Shabbat* 'table' *a la Bobov,* or *a la Belz.* It is much more difficult to talk about those things a Rebbe does on the inside, in the higher regions, working on him or herself, and with others! As a Rebbe by vocation, Hannah Rohel of Ludmir had to force the work of the *Shekhinah*, the "divine Feminine,' out into the open. *Barukh ha'Shem*, this is less difficult now, and there are more women with this vocation who are free to do the work in the open. But the question is still—How do you do that? What do you do?

So I want you to understand that what I have put into books like *Spiritual Intimacy* and *Sparks of Light*, I had to scrape together myself and gather from my own life's experience. And it is this that I have to offer you. I cannot claim to have all the pieces, or all the ingredients; but I pray that the *Shekhinah* will find ways to give us what is missing, so that nothing essential will be lacking.

Hasid <—> Rebbe

A long time ago, I wrote an article called "Hasidism and Neo-Hasidism," where I spoke of Hasid as a relationship word like 'son' or 'daughter,' 'father' or 'mother.' Just as you can't be a son or daughter without a father or a mother, you can't be a Hasid without a Rebbe. So, if somebody says to me, "I'm a Hasid," I want to know, "Who is your Rebbe?" It's the same in other traditions, like Sufism. If you say you are a Sufi, then I will ask, "Who is your Murshid?" Because, it is not possible to have one axis of the relationship without the other.

Once, Reb Moshe Kobriner was stopped by an old companion from his childhood who said to him: "Reb Moshe, I know you from way back; what do I have to believe about you in order to be your Hasid and you to be my Rebbe?" And Reb Moshe responded: "All you have to believe is that I'm a—*kletz'l hekher fun dir*—like a tree stump, that I'm just that much higher than you; that's all you need to believe. But if you don't believe there is some difference, that what I have to offer comes from a little higher point-of-view, you won't receive it." That is to say, it won't flow down to you; the *hashpa'ah*, or 'guidance' won't come down. So this is something to consider.

Hierarchy

Do not mistake me—I am not advocating the continuance of rigid hierarchy. Hierarchy is like a pyramid with a point on top and nearly all of its mass below. We are still suffering and being choked by hierarchies today. In a hierarchy, the person on top often refuses to listen to those below, despite their numerical majority. A message sent up to the top is rarely received. In the history of Catholicism, how often has the Vatican really responded to the needs of the rank and file priests and their congregations? Too often, they didn't want to hear it. Likewise, our government is also choked by its hierarchies. Think of healthcare, welfare and education—the patients, the needy and our children are so clearly on the bottom of the pyramid, and the people who deliver it are on the top. Can you imagine how much of the budgets for these services gets absorbed by the officials on the top, how many people live on the backs of those they're supposed to help? They get their big salaries and comparatively little trickles down to the person the system is meant to serve. So, I am not an advocate of having a Rebbe sitting on top of a big hierarchy—that's not what I am suggesting.

In the past, there were many such hierarchical situations in Hasidism. For instance, someone once asked Reb Yisrael, the Rhyzhiner Rebbe, "How can you spend the money that the Hasidim give you as a *mitzvah* on grand horses and a carriage?" He answered, "I have three kinds of Hasidim who give me money; and with that money, I *raise them up*. That is to say, I do something with the money to help them. From the contributions of the best Hasidim, I buy a *lulav* and *etrog* and a *sefer Torah,* and everything that has to do with learning and *mitzvot*. From the middlin' Hasidim, I keep the household going. And from the contributions of those who are less committed to their own spiritual welfare, but who still want me to raise them up in some way and connect them, I buy the horses and the like. So, you see, I have a lot of these Hasidim."

Now that is a very clear hierarchical statement.

Organismic

What is the alternative? Everybody is equal. But if everybody is equal, then there is no flow and things tend to stagnate. Alan Watts used to speak of the *Tao* as the "Watercourse Way," for water flows downward. If you understand this as a principle, then you know there has to be a certain amount of the hierarchical situation. Inside, I personally feel—"More than the calf wants to suck, the cow wants to give the milk," as it says in the Talmud (Pesahim 112a). Especially at this time in my life, I feel it is so important to 'upload' the files of my life's experience to others. So the pressure is very great.

On your side, the longing for the knowledge is also great. So you understand that we are in this wonderful relationship with each other. And it is not like the 'flatland' of democracy. So, what is it? Not pyramid, not hierarchy, not flatland, not democracy. I call it 'organismic.' I really want you to hear that because I think it is the foundation of the new Rebbework. The kidneys have to do the work of the kidneys in our organism. The lungs have to do the work of the lungs. The brain has to do the work of the brain. The spine has to do the work of the spine. The heel has to do the work of the heel. This doesn't mean that my toe doesn't have access to my head . . . Step on it and you'll see! Messages go both up and down in the organism. And just like the body, we are all organically connected.

In the past, people often used the familiar model of monarchy: a great king with a host of advisors, the *melekh ma'lkhai ham'lakhim,* with the *pamalya shel ma'lah,* the heavenly family *(pamalya = familia).* The Latin, *famulus,* includes more than the wife and children, but also the servant, the family pet, down to the mouse in the mouse hole and the cheese. The Hebrew *shifhah* is 'maidservant'; *mishpaḥa* is 'family.' So in this *familia shel ma'lah* there are angels and archangels and other orders of being, and they all have a place in the hierarchy of the monarchial model.

Thus, the Rebbe was seen as the *nassi',* or 'prince,' and the people around him, *m'kuravvim,* 'advisors,' and *gaba'im,* 'attendants.' There were also grades for the Rebbes, too. There is a wonderful book by Gershon Kranzler called *Williamsburg Memories* in which he describes the hierarchy of Rebbes— *Eynikl Rebbe, Shtikl Rebbe, Sheyner Yid,* and a regular Hasid, down to a worker, a *balabus,* a *yungerman,* a *bokher* and a *yingale.* That's the way they saw the hierarchy.

But my sense is that the stability of the Hasidic court is no longer desirable or possible. In the organic connection of the next paradigm, in which Gaia brings us the organismic model, Earth is alive and we are all a part of her, cells that make up the organs, organs that make up an organism, an organism that makes up a social organism with other organisms and the environment. That is the organismic model—which is superior to both pyramidic hierarchy and the flatland of democracy.

Rebbe or Rasha'?

We don't have many *tzaddikim* today. We are mostly *r'sha'im sheinam g'murim,* 'people who are not entirely bad,' who have been called to do this work. Nor do we have all the tools that are necessary to do it; but, *b'ḥemlat ha'Shem,* with the help of God, we are doing what we can, picking up *pranayama* and *asana,* breath work and postures, and spiritual direction from anywhere we can find it—trying to make up for the pieces we have lost. We are also getting ingredients from our past and experimenting to find the practices necessary for our future—transformational psychologies which have to do with the mind-science and the expansion of consciousness, allowing us to conceive of larger possibilities, having to do with local networks of people who work in dyads and triads, enmeshing consciousness to collaborate for greater ends. These things are on the horizon, so try to incorporate them and bring them into your work. You will need them.

Longing for the Holy

How did you come to want to hear these teachings? Had you been inspired by someone or something else? When my friend, Reb Shlomo Carlebach, would speak to a crowd of people, you would often see faces filled with a kind of exaltation. For a moment, each of them had ceased to be an *I* and become part of a larger *We.* That was Reb Shlomo's genius—he was a master of 'virtuous reality.' He could make people see that a virtuous reality was possible, and that created a powerful desire and yearning in them to live in that reality. In that moment, you feel part of the larger *We,* and the potency of the experience creates a longing in you. Having felt so much bigger, you want to inhabit that larger *We-body* again, to make it a reality again.

Sometimes when you teach, or give a sermon or lead services, you can feel that *We-inflation*. You feel that you are bigger, larger than life, in direct line with the prophets, the Rebbes and saints, and you feel—*"Oy! I am called to do this! I need to do this! I want to do this!"* But, the truth is, you are not always in that We-inflation. Sometimes you are the needy one; there still is a hurt child on the inside crying, and you can see how easy it is to make mistakes, to think that you are entitled to act on the childish greed in you, the lust you have, precisely because of the inflated vision you had of yourself before. So, do you see the problem of identification with the inflation?

To *Be* or Not to *Be* . . . a Rebbe

I've come to believe that the Rebbe of the future is not going to *be* a Rebbe. At times, he or she will *serve* as a Rebbe. And when that's done, that person will have a pizza and see a movie, and not necessarily *be* a Rebbe while doing so. The role and the task will not become one's entire being. Today, I came in as you know me, as the Reb Zalman you know. But you know what? I'm going to leave here afterward and I'll just be Zalman. Then, after the break, Reb Zalman will return and you'll want to stand until I sit down. I have an 'authority chair' to make that point also, to aid me in fulfilling the Rebbe-function.

I want to explain something about charisma. Without the group to put you into that place, without a listening ear, charisma may not flow so easily. So that tells us that some part of the charismatic effect is located outside of the individual to whom it is usually attributed; therefore, it may be given to whomever the group wishes. Thus, the 'authority chair' I mentioned might be yielded temporarily to another, and the group might allow that person to function for the group—provided that people will give an *ozen kashevet*, a 'hearing ear.' As Marc Antony says in Shakespeare's *Julius Caesar*, "Friends, Romans, countrymen, lend me your ears." *Ha'azinu*, 'ear me.' If you can get *that* 'loan,' it can be the 'down payment,' allowing the Rebbe in you to function temporarily.

Thinking of the Rebbe-function, I like to talk about 'role-play.' It is helpful to think of how we role-play Hasid and Rebbe. Not in the child's "let's pretend..." sense, but investing seriously in the roles on a temporary basis to allow something good to happen. Understanding that it is role-play that keeps us from getting stuck in the notion that we actually *are* the role we are playing. Instead, we understand that these are temporary roles we assume for the benefit of that mutuality which we are trying to create.

Charisma

How does this aspect of charisma work? I am standing here thinking—*What am I going to say next?* You are sitting there wondering—*What is he going to say next?* In this moment, the channel is open and you are feeding me a certain kind of energy, and that is so important to the function I am trying to perform.

There is a Zen *koan* about a flag that goes something like this: "Is the flag the cloth or the wind?" You see, to achieve the *function* of the flag, it is both the cloth and the wind interacting, inter-being. Is the river the water or the riverbed? It's both. The notion that I am speaking in the active form, and that you are merely passive, is wrong. Your active listening creates in me the will to continue. If there were a conspiracy

First Talk: Rebbe Training 101

among you to shut me out, to close your minds to me, in minutes my energy would collapse and I would be totally disconcerted—I wouldn't know what to do. How can I teach if you aren't paying attention. So it is clear that you are 'paying into' the process by offering me your attention.

If you withdrew your energy, I would probably stop and leave. I wouldn't have anything to do here. I am here only because you are helping me with your energy.

Moreover, when I come into this situation, I don't know what the group-mind will want to reveal. So I must also dedicate myself, at least for the time I am with a particular group or individual, to be a *keli,* a 'vessel' for what wants to come through me from the group-mind.

This is very important. The carrier wave for the message comes from the world of *Assiyah,* the world of action, but not the physical *Assiyah.* You are offering the energy. If I were to say it, using a Yiddish word, it might come out like this—You *fargin* me! *Farginen* is the very opposite of begrudging; it is to wish one the best, to send energy in a very positive way.

When I was in Amsterdam, I saw a sign that said *Volledige Vergunning,* meaning, 'total *farginen.*' So I said to somebody—"I want such a sign for my office! That way, every time I feel depleted, I can look at that sign and I know that, at least from the side of the *Ribbono shel 'Olam,* I get *Volledige Vergunning!*"

The fact that you *'fargin* me' is helping me to give you what you want. You are giving me energy, and I am giving it back to you with a manifest message, so that it becomes a carrier wave that carries the message.

Love is the strongest carrier wave: I experience love from you, and I give that love back to you with a message.

Love—the Carrier Wave

In teaching, I am sending love to all of you; in a sense, I'm making love with you. And in your looks, I see your response to that love. Now, can you understand what this does to the heart of a person when there is confusion about that response? That is to say, if the teacher interprets the positive response as being a love-response to the teacher's identity and not to the teaching function? It can contaminate the situation and spill over into inappropriate behavior. We learned the hard way about that in the 1960s and 70s.

So the understanding that there is a carrier wave of love going back and forth between us is clear, and this love is in the service of *teaching/learning*. On top of that love can come the information, the teaching itself. But something remarkable happens when this information is delivered on a carrier wave of love.

Sometimes I tune in to one of the televangelists on television and turn off the sound to see what they are really telegraphing. For instance, they might be talking about 1st Corinthians 13 on love, and yet, they are making angry or judgmental faces. So even though the information might be about love, the carrier wave is not a loving one.

A person's look carries a message. And the look can be a gift. When I saw the Bobover Rebbe, Rabbi Shlomo Halberstam, saying Torah, his look was saying: "I'll give you the very best I have to give; I want you to receive goodness." In other words, the carrier wave was love.

There are wonderful stories of how the Ba'al Shem Tov sometimes reproved itinerant preachers who came into small towns, putting the *"fear of God"* into simple Jews over all the wrongs that they had done, when they were just trying to eke out a living and be decent Jews. So the Ba'al Shem Tov would say to the preachers: "Why don't you start giving God a hard time instead of these good people? After all, He isn't meeting their needs either!" With this, he was also saying that the carrier wave needed to be love.

Different Kinds of Love

Charisma operates in a setting that C.S. Lewis describes in *The Four Loves* as *agápe*. There, Lewis uses the four Greek words for love to explain about the different types of love we experience. (We also have them in Hebrew to some extent.)

On the lowest level is *storge*, 'affection,' the fondness we have for something or someone, simply because of familiarity.

Then there is *philia*, 'friendship,' the genuine liking we have for something or someone. When you talk about a bibliophile, you are talking about a person who really likes books, who has a genuine interest in them—reading them, caring for them, appreciating the aesthetics of them, *et cetera*. A Freudian analyst would tell you that the person has a book *cathexis,* meaning that the person has invested libido energy in books. If you were to take a book from that person and tear it up, it would almost cause them physical pain because they have invested loving energy in their books.

After that comes *eros*, the love between individuals, which might range from powerful sexual desire, the urge for Life, to the romantic love we call 'being in love.'

Finally, there is *agápe*. To explain this, let me give you a little New Testament teaching:

Jesus says to Peter, "Do you love *(agápu)* me?"

And Peter says, "Yes, I do—I love *(philio)* you."

"Do you love *(agápu)* me?" Jesus asks again.

"I love *(philio)* you," Peter declares.

"Do you love *(agápu)* me?" Jesus asks one last time.

"I love *(philio)* you," says Peter. (John 21:15-19)

You see, when you just read it in English, you miss what is really going on here. *Agápe* is unconditional love. So Jesus is asking, "Do you love me unconditionally?" And Peter is answering, "I really like you!" And later we find when Jesus is in a bad way, Peter betrays him three times.

Agápe is also *'us'* love. There are times on *Shabbat* morning when I look around and I see how we love one another and I really love *us!* But we must be careful with that kind of love, because there is a shadow side to it. A *mitnagged,* an 'opponent' of Hasidism once put it this way: In Hebrew, the stork is called ḥasidah; and about it is said, *M'shum sh'hiy' mitḥasedet rak im ḥavereiha,* "She is only nice to her own and not to others." Sadly, this is true of many Hasidim. They have *agápe* for those within their circle, but not for those outside of it.

But there is one more kind of love—*charis,* from which we get the word, charity. *Charis* is a love that is rooted in compassion. It is the Sacred Heart of Jesus in Catholic Christianity and the *maha-karuna,* or 'great compassion' of Mahayana Buddhism. In Judaism, we speak of *ahavah rabbah,* the 'great love.' It is for everyone. When the Ba'al Shem Tov would speak of *ahavat Yisrael,* the love of his fellow Jews, there were still *agápe* boundaries there. But *charis* is even for the *goyim,* the 'nations.'

Not long ago, on the second day of Tammuz, I went to spend

time with the Habad Hasidim in Boulder for the Lubavitcher Rebbe's *yahrzeit* and was pleasantly surprised to hear one of my old Lubavitcher colleagues, Reb Manis Friedman, the founder of the Bais Chana Women International, talking about how important it is to include *goyim* in that love!

The seventh Lubavitcher Rebbe once said, "When you are sitting in a plane, turn to whoever is sitting next to you and start talking to them about keeping the seven *mitzvot* of the children of Noah." I tell you, I was greatly moved when I heard that; because, for the first time, it seemed, we were not rejecting non-Jews.

All this is to say, the love must be as large as possible, reaching the level of *charis*.

Royal Jelly

Now I am going to come in for a landing on this topic.

We need Rebbes, and we need to find a way to feed the 'royal jelly' to our fellow Jews. After the first two generations of Hasidism, the royal jelly of deep spiritual guidance was mostly given only to the children of Rebbes, to solidify the dynastic situation. Only rarely in the later period did someone like Rabbi Ahrele Roth, an ordinary Hasid, become a Rebbe, grabbing a jar of royal jelly from the court of his master, the Bluzhover Rebbe. Now, in our day, we have to take hold of the jar in the same way.

I want to make clear that, although we are not *tzaddikim*, and we are not Rebbes as we have seen them in the past, there are those among us who are called to *function* as Rebbes. We recognize that this is not a permanent situation or role, but an intermittent function to which we submit in order to be able to provide access for others to regions beyond ordinary consciousness. And if we want Judaism and our people to be healthy, we can't do it without people who will function as the conduits of that expanded consciousness.

Question and Answer Session

Question: My sense is that something is probably lost if someone is only "functioning as a Rebbe" temporarily, even if the vertical connection is good at that time. So the question is—What are we missing by not being in the traditional sociological context of Hasidism in which the Rebbe is expected to be 'connected' all the time?

Reb Zalman: In the past, in that sociological context, it was easier to be a *tzaddik* or 'saint,' because you didn't do anything but *tzaddik* all day long. Your world and your life was much more circumscribed and your vertical connection was built on a scaffold of support made up of many other people and cultural values. Today, there are more demands on our time and attention, and our lives and worlds are much more diverse. So, while we may not easily be able to go so high as they did, we have an advantage in breadth and our horizontal connections.

In the past, the *tzaddik* was often thought of as a tall, solitary tree like a redwood. But the tradition also says, *tzaddik katamar yif'rah k'erez bal'vanon yis'geh*, "A *tzaddik* is like a blossoming date-palm." (Ps. 92:13) Now, date-palms are usually found in pairs, male and female. A redwood, on the other hand, while very tall, stands alone. And while a redwood might reach greater heights, date-palms, which live in pairs, produce lots of fruit. Both are *tzaddikim*.

What is necessary for us, living more in the horizontal situation, is to learn as much as we can about the various masculine and feminine connections available to us. There is a wonderful teaching by Reb Hayyim of Tchernovitz in his *Be'er Mayim Hayyim* about the four who entered into *Pardes:*

Ben Azzai died because he wasn't married and anchored to someone below; Ben Zoma, who was a widower, lost his mind when he saw his wife in Paradise and had to return to Earth; Elisha ben Abuya was divorced and thus was open to 'cutting his roots' in Judaism; Rabbi Akiva was the only one who was happily married and thus able to return from the *Pardes* in peace. Before making his 'ascent,' he and his wife Rahel made love; and when he returned, they did so again. So it was from that place that he went to the *Pardes,* and to that place he returned. Thus, his going and coming were very peaceful, safe and grounded.

So that is *tzaddik katamar yif'rah,* "A *tzaddik* is like a blossoming date-palm." But there is also the element of *k'erez bal'vanon yis'geh,* "they thrive like a cedar in Lebanon." Lebanon is *lev,* 'heart,' and the letter *nun,* whose numerical equivalent is fifty, is related to *binah* and the "Fifty Gates of Understanding." So there is a connection; the heart is awake and full of openness and understanding.

Question: People seem to have forgotten how to treat spiritual leaders with respect; how can we begin to change this situation?

Reb Zalman: You may have to model the behavior yourself, inviting a guest to speak and demonstrating the proper way to treat a guest for them. It is very important to do that. Spiritual leaders need to show respect and give honor to one another first. They cannot be tearing one another down. That will be a beginning; and, God willing, the rest will follow.

But people also need to know that this respect is not about elitism or some outmoded etiquette. This respect helps one to maintain a focus and preserves an atmosphere beneficial for the teaching that needs to happen. In the past, when I would lead retreats at Fellowship House and Farm in Pennsylvania, I often had to help in the work of setting things up, because these things weren't already taken care of. And, while I was doing this, people would come up to me and ask questions of the Rebbe. But I would have to say, "The Rebbe isn't here yet; right now, you're talking to the *shammes*, the 'servant.' "

It is impossible to do deep Rebbe-work if you have to be the *shammes* at the same time. If you are expecting deep teaching from someone, you have to give them time to get there, to connect with the *shalshelet*, with the chain of their transmission; you have to support them in their spiritual practice, providing an atmosphere and a situation supportive of the result you want.

Second Talk

The Soul-Cluster of the Rebbe

I WANT TO BEGIN with a *b'rakhah*, a 'blessing':

May the leaders among you find it easy, when the time comes, to receive in your body that gift that people give you when they rise out of respect; that you are able to receive it without the contamination of ego-inflation, but are able to give it back in *b'rakhot*, in 'blessings.' I pray that your *talmidim*, your 'students,' will value your expenditure of energy on the work to which you have dedicated yourselves.

May you be given the blessing of being able to avoid having to say, as Moses did, *Eikha essa le'vadi tor'ḥakhem u'mas'akhem v'riv'khem*, "How will I bear your troubles, your burdens and your arguments!" (Deut. 1:12) And may you find that you have *shishim gibborim*, 'sixty mighty warriors' to protect you, as they did the bed of King Solomon, as the Ba'al Shem Tov demanded before agreeing to enter the world to teach his message.

It is interesting to look around at the *shishim gibborim* who surround me now, the *talmidim*, the 'students' who "are here, and those who are not here today," and to see how alive they are in their *Yiddishkeit*, in their Judaism.

But being alive with Judaism doesn't mean your relationship with it is perfect. Life is messy! When God gives us a baby, we have to do a lot of diaper changing; and what we are doing is still in its infancy, so there will still be lots of diapers to change. Anytime we really engage life, engaging it in a vital way, with enthusiasm, we make lots of mistakes. But that's how we learn; and often a lot of beauty comes from those mistakes. So, whenever we see something that doesn't quite measure-up among our companions, and in ourselves, we should think of *na'ar Yisrael,* the baby of Israel taking its first wobbly steps. We are still so young in this paradigm, and there is still so much to learn, to catch up on from the past, to find our bearings in the present, and to prepare for the work of the future.

The General Soul

I want to talk about *neshamot klaliyot,* 'aggregate souls.'

A Rebbe is sometimes described as *Rosh B'nai Yisrael (RB"I),* the 'head of the children of Israel.' But the way I think of a Rebbe is as a *neshamah klalit,* a 'general soul,' intimately connected with a number of other souls who look to that person for guidance.

For Lubavitcher Hasidim in this generation, there is no question that the Rebbe, Rabbi Menachem Mendel Schneersohn, is the *neshamah klalit* who connects them all. But it is also important to understand that *neshamot klaliyot,* 'aggregate souls' do not have to be holy beings, *tzaddikim,* like the Rebbe; they can also be *resha'im,* people who do evil in the world. So even though the *lashon kodesh,* the 'holy language' rebels at the association, it is clear that Adolf Hitler was also a kind of *neshamah klalit* for many people.

You see, the idea of a *neshamah klalit* is not necessarily about good or evil, it is about a function a person fulfills. Thus, when we look back at the day John F. Kennedy was killed, and see

Second Talk: The Soul-Cluster of the Rebbe

how many people were utterly distraught, it is clear that he was functioning as a *neshamah klalit* for those people.

It is not that the *neshamah klalit* 'owns' the souls who are connected to his or her general soul, but that he or she is the common connecting-point and symbol for a group.

How did the people who now associate themselves with Jewish renewal come to think of themselves as a group? I had been traveling all over the United States and Canada, giving lectures and talks, conducting a *Shabbaton* here and a *Shabbaton* there, and thus became the connection between the people who had heard these talks and attended these events. In one town, I would naturally suggest that one person get in touch with someone else in another town, and before you know it, there is a kind of network of souls across the country, a *hevrah* connected to one another and to me. Thus, the *neshamah klalit* could be seen as the 'convener,' or that which brings people together. It is a function and a task, not an elite rank or position.

A *Karass* or Soul-Cluster

In Kurt Vonnegut's *Cat's Cradle,* he coins a wonderfully useful term for a cluster of souls, calling them a *karass*. In the book, he creates a fictional religion called Bokononism, and has two Bokononians going through a death-bed ritual, repeating the Last Rites:

> God made mud.
>
> God got lonesome.
>
> So God said to some of the mud, "Sit up!"
>
> "See all I've made," said God, "the hills, the sea, the

sky, the stars."

And I was some of the mud that got to sit up and look around.

Lucky me, lucky mud.

I, mud, sat up and saw what a nice job God had done.

What interesting other kinds of sitting-up mud I met!

Then, as he is getting ready to die, he says:

I loved everything I saw!

Good night.

I will go to heaven now.

I can hardly wait . . .

To find out for certain what my *wampeter* was . . .

And who was in my *karass* . . .

And all the good things our *karass* did for you.

Amen.[1]

A *karass*, in Vonnegut's fictional religion, is a destiny-group, in which all the people who are our friends and enemies, all the people with whom we have intimate connections and difficult issues, are connected.

What I want to say is that there is a sense in which a *neshamah klalit* is also a *karass*. It is not just a 'general soul' with numerous connections, but it is also a 'soul-cluster' for which

---

[1] Kurt Vonnegut, *Cat's Cradle* (1963), 99.

one person, the Rebbe, often serves as a symbol, or better yet, as the 'sysop' of a 'bulletin board.' In Internet terminology, a sysop is a 'systems operator' who handles a particular on-line bulletin board, helping users to navigate and deal with issues as they come up.

My sense is that we may also belong to more than one *neshamah klalit* at a time, to more than one soul-cluster. Think about it this way: if you're a sports fan, a football fan, and you like the New York Giants, you're part of that *neshamah klalit*. Among music fans, I also know of people who belong to the *neshamah klalit* of the Grateful Dead! And you might be both at the same time.

For some people, these connections are very powerful and create a *participation mystique* and a kind of shared consciousness. It is a whole social-body pursuing a shared goal with some entity at the center, into which each person can 'plug-in.' And these are just common examples. You might also think of political parties, cause-oriented groups, cultures, religions, *et cetera*.

The Destiny-Group Paradox

Now, I have been talking about different ways to understand the *neshamah klalit*, but the traditional understanding is of a specific, unchanging 'destiny-group,' i.e., you are always a part of the same 'soul-network,' as it were. But I'm not so sure. I feel that people are sometimes a part of one *neshamah klalit* and then another, that there may be some *karass*-shifting going on. I feel the *Shekhinah*, the 'Divine Presence,' is stirring the pot of genetic and soul-inheritance a lot more now than was done in the past.

Rabbi Hayyim Vital, the great kabbalist and disciple of the holy AR"I, was dealing with this in a way when addressing the question of *gilgul* or 'reincarnation' in a world of increasing population. If reincarnation is about dealing with our *karma* from past incarnations, and if it is possible to reach a point at which we no longer need to be reincarnated, then why do we have more people in the world today than we had in the past? It should be the other way around; in every generation, a few more people drop out, their souls having completed their journey. It's a good question.

So what's the answer? *History is accelerating,* and in order for us to finish our reincarnational work, some of us have to have parallel incarnations. That is to say, the *neshamah* breaks into separate *neshamot,* different clusters, as it were, of which each *neshamah pratit,* each 'specific soul,' does the specific job it has to do, like a parallel processor. There are some computers called 'connection machines' that have 4,000 CPUs working in concert together, crunching numbers at the same time, so that the results come in much quicker. Also, with an extended life span, there is the possibility of doing more 'business' in one lifetime, dealing with many different souls in different periods of one's life.

The main point I want to get across is that the *neshamah klalit* is not an architectural notion that necessarily stands fast forever, but is an evolving field. Perhaps we should think less in terms of specific reincarnations, and more of the re-souling of matter!

Second Talk: The Soul-Cluster of the Rebbe

Transpersonal Psychology & Transpersonal Sociology

When Transpersonal Psychology first came on the scene, it was a fantastic liberation; it lifted the ceiling off the cortex and rational mentality, and allowed us to move into higher, more subtle areas of intuition.

It was as if to say: besides the Judaism of Earth, of action and materiality; besides the Judaism of Water, of feeling, emotionality; and besides the Judaism of Air, of mind and intellect, we also needed the Judaism of Fire, of divine intuition.

Ha'Shem Elohekha aish okhlah hu, "Ha'Shem, our God, is a consuming fire." (Deut. 4:24) How can we approach God if God is a consuming fire unless we are also, in some sense, fire? We are a *nitzutz*, a divine 'spark,' a *ḥelek Elohah mi'ma'al*, a 'part of the divine being.' Fire does not have to fear fire.

Because transpersonal psychology was open to the transcendent and trans-personal, and not limited to the merely personal—to the mind, emotions and body—it could also take the sacred traditions of the East and West into consideration. It could take the experiences of St. John of the Cross into consideration when he speaks of entering the "dark night," where he knew knowledge that surpassed the mind. What does it mean? How did he know, if not with sensation, feeling or reason? The answer is *intuition*.

Through Transpersonal Psychology, intuition became kosher for everyone. What we are missing is a transpersonal sociology and a transpersonal politics. When the 14th Dalai Lama and I were talking in Dharamsala, it became so clear to me that this was not simply a conversation happening on this plane alone, the *Sar shel Yahadut* and the *Sar shel Tibet*—the 'angel of the Jews' and the 'angel of the Tibetans'—were also having a conversation; on this plane, we were enacting what was happening on another plane.[2]

In a sense, this is what is necessary for us to consider. Nobody thinks about what is necessary to make peace and a *tikkun* between the Bosnians and Serbs on other levels, because we are not yet open to the idea of a transpersonal sociology dealing with the soul-clusters, the *neshamot klaliyot* of different peoples and cultures, and the *sarim* or 'angels' who represent them in the upper worlds. If we want to contribute to a *tikkun olam*, a 'rectification of the world,' in a really powerful way, we have to do it with an awareness of transpersonal sociology and transpersonal politics.

I often say, "The only way to get it together . . . is together." Because no one can get it together for someone else. It takes *together-ing* to get it together. If the world is to heal, it will take a number of people doing their spiritual work together on a higher level, and that is still largely unexplored territory.

The Root of the Soul

We need our Rebbes to work on these different levels, and with the Hasidim of their soul-cluster too, discerning whether the root of a Hasid's soul is actually connected with them or not. You see, as a *neshamah klalit*, it is critically important to discern whether one actually has the *shoresh ha'neshamah*, the root of a potential disciple's soul, to know if they are really connected, and how deeply connected.

There have been many people over the years who have asked me to serve them as their Rebbe, and after talking with them

---

[2] Rodger Kamenetz, *The Jew in the Lotus* (1994), 72-90.

Second Talk: The Soul-Cluster of the Rebbe

for a while, I have had to say, "No, I don't have your *shoresh ha'neshamah* with me." That is to say, I find that we do not have the right kind of compatibility, and that I cannot generate the kind of pastoral concern I might have for others. That does *not* mean that I do not like the person, that I am profiling for particular personality traits or discriminating against others. It simply means that there is no pastoral heart-connection on my end. And in this case, I feel it is better for these people to find other teachers with whom they will have a better connection. Intimacy is spiritual, and sometimes it just isn't there.

And yet, there have been many others where the connection was clear, and the distinct feeling of pastoral concern pervades the relationship from the beginning. But even in this situation, it is not a matter of personal tastes. How can I say it? There are some *talmidim*, some 'students' who rub my psyche the wrong way on occasion, and sometimes often; but it is still clear that they are my *talmidim*, that their *shoresh ha'neshamah* is mine to deal with. I continue to feel concern for them despite my personal annoyances and am able to function as a *neshamah klalit* for them. And they may likewise feel a similar rub with me. This is what it is to be part of a destiny-group.

It is also possible to be wrong about such connections. Sometimes you have to give it a little time. There have been some people whom I have *wanted* to help, to rescue, and some who have 'conned' me into thinking we *might* have a connection, but it eventually becomes clear and I don't feel any great loss. Whereas, I would certainly feel a grieving loss if someone who was really connected to me at the root of the soul were to move away from me.

There are also lateral connections between co-workers on the spiritual path, spiritual friendships and collaborations, as well as tangential hierarchical connections—temporary or short-term connections, connections that are more limited in scope—more avuncular relationships.

When I first visited the Bobover Rebbe, Rabbi Shlomo Halberstam, for *Simḥat Torah* and *Sh'mini Atzeret (Shabbat B'reshit),* I so enjoyed it that I came to see him the next day with a *kvittel,* a 'petitionary note' and said: "I already have a Rebbe. I'm a Lubavitcher Hasid. However, I also feel good coming here, and I would like to do this with your permission. I don't want to feel like I'm coming to 'steal' from you. I only want to share the warmth."

He responded with a gentle smile and said: "One may have an apple tree that bears Macintosh apples; but if one grafts a sprig from a Golden Delicious apple tree to it, in time it will grow to be part of that tree and bear fruit also. And from the Golden Delicious branch will come Golden Delicious apples, and from the main tree branches will come Macintosh apples."

Then he assumed a very familiar manner of speech and said, "Your father is a Galicianer (a Hasid from the region of Galicia), is he not?"

I said, "Yes."

Then he mused, "Toss a stick in the air and it falls on its root!" In other words, the apple doesn't fall far from the tree—Bobov is a Hasidic lineage from Galicia.

In other words, he discerned something about my *shoresh ha'neshamah* and recognized a kind of avuncular connection between us. This is something essential to discern when you are dealing with someone who wants to work with you on a deeper level.

Second Talk: The Soul-Cluster of the Rebbe

Discerning the Reflection of The Archetypal Human Potential

But there is another discernment which concerns the *shoresh ha'neshamah* that has to do with spiritual guidance. This is something I'll discuss at greater length later, but I want to bring it up and establish it in the context of what I have just said about the connection between a teacher and a disciple.

I wish I were able to say that I had very conscious and deliberate access to psychic gifts, but I do not. Nevertheless, I have a relationship with my intuition that I depend on to guide me in my prayer-life and in my relations with my *talmidim*. I used to have a box in which I kept photos of my students, and I would pray over those photos once a month before Rosh Hodesh. And occasionally, I would stop on a particular photo, feeling a special concern, and would later call them to find out how they were. So even though I cannot claim to be looking at these people who are connected with me in terms of deliberate psychic awareness, the bond that I have with them, on the level of transpersonal sociology, does make me aware of certain needs on the level of intuition.

When it comes to spiritual guidance in *yehidut*, in the 'encounter' between a Rebbe and Hasid, it is also necessary to connect to and discern something from the root of the Hasid's soul. According to the Mittler Rebbe, Rabbi Dov Baer of Lubavitch, it is necessary to see the person as "reflected in the primordial thought of *Adam Kadmon*." He says:

> When my father placed this task on my shoulders, he said to me, "The proper way to look at a person (in *yehidut*) is to see them as they are reflected in the primordial thought of *Adam Kadmon*."

I learned three things from these words:

The soul as it is reflected in the primordial thought is on the level of a 'child.' When it descends and becomes invested in a body, it is more like a 'servant.' But since I was charged to see a person as they stand in the primordial thought, I learned that the soul can be a 'child' even in its lowest descent.[3]

That is to say, a Rebbe needs to look at the Hasid as one would look upon a child, as being full of unmanifest potential and basking in the unconditional love of God, as "reflected in the primordial thought of *Adam Kadmon*," the archetype of all human potential. Looking at the original template and design, the Rebbe is better able to proscribe for the Hasid.

How does this work? It is not something that can be done without altering one's state of consciousness and developing a strong relationship with one's own intuition. When I see someone for spiritual counseling in *yeḥidut*, I have to find the person's question or problem, *b'dakkut d'dakkut*, 'in the most subtle way' inside of myself. You see, it is only when I can fix it inside of me that I am able to help them.

I remember one occasion where I saw a young man who was struggling to get over a debilitating fear that was keeping him from living up to his potential. He told me his basic problem; but I couldn't feel it in my body yet, so I asked him to describe it again. He described it in different terms; but again, nothing. So this time I asked him to go into a memory connected with the fear and describe it to me in detail. He thought for a moment and told me that a dream was coming to him instead. He began to tell me the dream in detail and I was soon able to

---

[3] Zalman Schachter-Shalomi and Netanel Miles-Yépez, *A Hidden Light: Stories and Teachings of Early HaBaD and Bratzlav Hasidism* (2011), 180.

feel in myself the echo of what he was feeling, and with it, an intuition about how to deal with his particular issue.

Compassionate Rebbe-hood

But it isn't just a matter of spiritual imagination and intuition; a Rebbe must have a deep concern and compassion for a Hasid. Two related anecdotes from the HaBaD tradition come to mind.

The sons of fourth Lubavitcher Rebbe, Zalman Aharon and his brother Shalom Dov Baer are playing 'Rebbe and Hasid.' The older brother, Zalman Aharon says, "I'll be the Rebbe, and you'll be my Hasid. This will be my study."

So Shalom Dov Baer, 'the Hasid,' goes out and ties a *gartel* or 'payer sash' around his waist, and then knocks gently on the door. Hearing, "Enter!" he comes back in through the door, kisses the *mezuzah,* and humbly says to his older brother, "Rebbe, I need a *tikkun,* a 'fixing' for my *neshamah,* for my 'soul.' "

"What have you done?" asks his brother, 'the Rebbe.'

Shalom Dov Baer, just five years old answers, "I stole a pickle from mother."

Hearing this, his brother, Zalman Aharon, who was seven years old, laughed out loud. "That's not a sin—mother will be happy that you're eating!"

But Shalom Dov Baer, who hadn't asked permission and felt bad about it, looked troubled and said, "You're not a Rebbe."

"Why do you say that?" Zalman Aharon asks.

"Because," says Shalom Dov Baer, "A Rebbe never laughs at

the pain of a Hasid."

On another occasion, they're playing the same game and Shalom Dov Baer comes in and says, "I need a *tikkun*—I forgot to make a *b'rakhah*, a 'blessing' over the food I ate."

"Well," says Zalman Aharon, "that's simple. For the next forty days you are to recite a *b'rakhah* out of the *siddur*, the 'prayer-book,' after eating any food.

But Shalom Dov Baer says, "You didn't do it right."

"What do you mean?" says Zalman Aharon, "We both saw Papa through the keyhole giving a Hasid this same *tikkun* over the same sin!"

His little brother answered, "Yes, but Papa always sighs before answering."

These little episodes proved prophetic, because it was the younger brother, Shalom Dov Baer who became the fifth Lubavitcher Rebbe.

Discerning the Needs of the Individual

In the next talk, I want discuss the needs of the individual and how to discern individual differences. In the work of spiritual leadership, it is very important to be able to know what kind of person you are dealing with.

Back when I wrote my first little booklet on meditation, *The First Step*, which was later added to *The First Jewish Catalog*, I was so convinced that everyone had to follow a particular route—'first you do this, then you do that'—as it is in the *M'sillat Y'sharim* of Moshe Hayyim Luzzatto. There you begin with *zehirut*, 'watchfulness,' and proceed to *z'rizut*, 'diligence,' and from there to *nekiyut*, 'cleanliness,' *et cetera*, step-by-step to the culmination of the path.

But the Ba'al Shem Tov says, *Y'sharim darkei Ha'Shem,* "Straightforward are the *ways* of God." Why does he say, "ways," plural? Because, sometimes a way is blocked and you have to go another way! Likewise, in Psalm 23:3, it says, *yan'ḥeini b'ma'ag'lei tzedek,* "God leads me in right paths." They may be circuitous, because you can't always go straight, but they are "right."

You have to know that not everybody needs to go the same route. Different personality and soul types have different needs. So it is very important to understand individual differences if you are going to be counseling and serving a group of people.

Question and Answer Session

Question: What is the significance of a *b'rakhah,* a 'blessing' from the Rebbe?

Reb Zalman: In the words of my father-in-law, a *b'rakhah* is like rain. If the soil is plowed and ready to be sown, and one throws seeds into the soil, the seeds will grow and blossom when rain falls upon them. If, however, the soil is unprepared, the seed finds difficulty in sprouting forth, even when there is an abundance of rain.

Rain can accomplish its function and be useful only when preceded by the plowing and tilling of the soil, planting of the seeds, and preparing the soil for growing. However, should rain fall on unplowed and untilled soil, not only won't it accomplish its function, but furthermore, it may cause damage.

The same applies to a *b'rakhah*. The body, the actions and desires of the body, must be tilled and plowed. Only then will the *b'rakhah* be useful and help the blessed to elevate themselves to a higher standard.

When an individual comes for a *b'rakhah* and is emotionally and spiritually equipped, the *b'rakhah* will help them to grow and blossom.

Question: In your talk, you presented the concept of the *neshamah klalit* in a way that suggested it is not something exclusively Jewish. I think there are many who would take issue with the idea that there could be *neshamot klaliyot* who were not *tzaddikim* from the Jewish tradition. What would you say to them?

Reb Zalman: Sometimes, I am bothered when people talk about the Ba'al Shem Tov's notion of *hashgahah pratit*, of 'specific divine providence,' where every leaf falling from a tree and turning in the wind has a purpose, and yet think that Jesus and the Buddha somehow escaped God's notice, as if such teachers, who affected millions of people for the good, were not important parts of God's plan for humanity.

Jesus and the Buddha are certainly *neshamot klaliyot*, access-points to Divinity, on a grand scale. We have to give up our triumphalism, the notion that our tradition is somehow superior to others. The same is true even *within* Judaism and Hasidism. Whether one is attached to the Lubavitcher Rebbe or the Satmarer Rebbe, all that is really important is that the connection to one or the other represents a relationship at the level of the *shoresh ha'neshamah*, at the 'root of one's soul.'

Second Talk: The Soul-Cluster of the Rebbe

Question: What are some of the sources in the Jewish tradition on reincarnation?

Reb Zalman: There is the *Sha'ar Ha'Gilgulim* and *Sefer Ha'Gilgulim* of Rabbi Hayyim Vital. Another interesting book is the *Seder Ha'Dorot* of Rabbi Yehiel Heilprin, which is a 'who's who' of incarnations. There you will find that Rabbi Akiva is an incarnation of Moshe *rabbeinu, et cetera,* and some strange associations. But you can also take a look at Simcha Raphael's excellent book, *Jewish Views of the Afterlife,* and my Foreword in it.

Third Talk

The Rebbe and Spiritual Typologies

OVER THE YEARS, as I have ordained new rabbis, I feel as if the difficult task of Jewish spiritual leadership left to those of us who were raised in the wake of the Holocaust is being distributed, and a great weight is slowly lifting. With God's help, this process will continue as we talk about the models of leadership found in the Hasidic tradition.

Principles of Education and Guidance

In 1943, my master, Rabbi Yosef Yitzhak Schneersohn, the sixth Lubavitcher Rebbe, traveled to Chicago and shared with the Hasidim there a treatise he had written in his youth called, *K'lalei Ha'Hinukh V'Ha'Hadrakhah*, 'Principles of Education and Guidance,' which I later translated into English.[4]

Treatises of this sort are unusual in Hasidism. Most Hasidic *sefarim* or 'books' are simply compilations of teachings and *obiter dicta* from the Rebbes that have been written down and later edited into a book. Usually, the editor would take the first sentence of the Rebbe's teaching and match it to a sentence in a particular portion of Torah, and then arrange all of the

---

[4] In 1898, when he was just 18 years old, his father, Rabbi Shalom Dov Baer of Lubavitch, asked him to write a discourse on education for a new Lubavitcher *yeshiva* and provided him with some of his own writings to be integrated into the text. He wrote two drafts based on these notes and completed the final draft that same year. However, the text was not published until 1944.

teachings according to the order of the *parshiot,* or Torah portions. Only seldom did a Rebbe intentionally compose a work like this one.

In it, my Rebbe writes about the theory of spiritual education and guidance and outlines its general principles. But he also looks at the educator or guide and talks about the self-examination he or she must do, asking questions like: "Am I seeing my students' needs clearly, or am I merely generalizing and talking about things that are particular to my own life and vision?" And this is what I want to talk about now—the proper appraisal of the student's needs.

The educator, to use the Rebbe's own terms, must be aware of the nature and qualities of the person who is on the receiving end of the education and guidance. More than that, he or she must also be aware of the environment in which the student lives and the circumstances of their life. The educator needs to have an understanding of what is "appropriate" and "inappropriate" for the student.

I like that he doesn't use the words "good" or "bad" here. After all, there may be things that are good in themselves, but which are inappropriate for the student to engage in at a given moment. When I was speaking to the Dalai Lama in Dharamsala, I noticed that he often said, "Very useful," which was his way of *not* saying, "Very good." Buddhism doesn't like to talk about good and bad as much as what is useful and what is not.

Later in the treatise, the Rebbe talks about choosing the right strategy for educating a particular person, and of prioritizing one's approach. That is to say, figuring out what needs to be done first, second, and so on.

He then talks about attributes that have to do with a person's essence, and attributes that are incidental to a person. And that is a very important distinction to make.

I can say to somebody, "You need to change!" And that is easily done with attributes that are not essential to a person. You simply exchange one habit for another; you move from one format to another. But when you are dealing with something essential to the person, it is a whole other problem, and not remotely simple. Therefore, it becomes critically important to be able to discern the type of person with whom you are dealing.

The Temperaments of the Cerebrotone, Somatotone and Viscerotone

In Aldous Huxley's classic book, *The Perennial Philosophy*, there is chapter called "Religion and Temperament" in which he talks about three types: the cerebrotone, the somatotone, and the viscerotone.

The *cerebrotone*, for the sake of classification, might be described as your stereotypical 'brainy' type—big head and Adam's apple—somewhat unconcerned with the rest of the body. If the cerebrotone didn't have to eat, they would be quite happy, because it is too often distracting them from their mental activities. But what are you going to do? You need to have a structure to hold the nervous system together so that there can be consciousness!

Then you have the *somatotone* who is always 'shoulder to the wheel,' 'nose to the grindstone,' 'do something,' 'what are you sitting around for?' There is no subject that amounts to beans if you aren't doing something about it. Their measure is always: 'I want to see what have you done . . . Show me your track record.'

Then there is the *viscerotone* who loves to hangout and celebrate with others, to relax, to sing and dance, to rejoice. If you ask the viscerotone about serving God, they'll tell you that you don't have to serve God . . . You need to *farbreng* with God, to hang-out with God, to worship and say *halleluyah!*

When I see Jesus depicted as this poor, emaciated man with his ribs sticking out, I sometimes challenge people to change their perspective and to see Jesus as a viscerotone. For instance, in the famous Matthias Grünewald crucifixion paintings of Jesus, we see him as a starved, tortured being, as if he were an ascetic. But that's not what we find in the Gospels. In Germany, I once saw a crucifixion painting where Jesus had a nice little belly. After all, what did his enemies say about him? That he was a *zolleil v'sovei* (Deut. 21:20), a "wine-bibber" and a "glutton." (Luke 7:34) And how did he begin his ministry? At a wedding, making wine! And what did he say at the end? Eat bread and drink wine in remembrance of me!

On the other hand, the Buddha, in the popular imagination, is often depicted as a viscerotone, with a big round belly, as a roly-poly, happy-go-lucky monk. But this is not the Buddha; it is actually a depiction of a Chinese Buddhist *bodhisattva* called Budai (or Hotei in Japan). The Buddha, at least before his enlightenment, was an extreme ascetic, a cerebrotone, doing all kinds of austerities, sometimes only eating a single grain of rice a day!

Moshe *rabbeinu*—Moses—is the one who is usually depicted most accurately. Think of Michelangelo's depiction of him as the law-giver. You can imagine him sitting there, being asked questions. "Moshe *rabbeinu*—what do you believe in?" He answers, as he does in Deuteronomy, "I believe in *doing* this"

Third Talk: The Rebbe and Spiritual Typologies

and "I believe in *doing* that." He's a somatotone! Judaism also comes out like this. Somebody says, "Can you tell me about the Jewish faith?" And we say, "We believe in keeping *Shabbat* and eating kosher, and in doing the *mitzvot*."

It often disturbs people, because they're interested in *pistis*, our cogitation about what it is, how we understand it in mental terms. But Jews have traditionally focused on *emunah*, usually translated as 'faith,' but which is very close to *imunim*, 'practice,' as in practicing on the piano. It has to do with *doing it* faithfully.[5]

So you see, there are types of personalities to be dealt with in the work of spiritual guidance, with different ways of seeing the world, and with different needs. The guide needs to be able to speak their different languages. And sometimes, to see how the cerebrotone needs a little more experience in the heart (viscerotone), or how the viscerotone needs to know how to think something through (cerebrotone) thoroughly.

Using Typologies

Is there such a thing as a pure type? No . . . a human being is far too complex to fit so neatly into a single category. There is no pure *hesed*, or 'loving-kindness' type—speaking in the language of Kabbalah—that doesn't also have all the other *sefirot* or 'qualities' in some measure. But it is interesting to see how people with similar tendencies and dispositions often have similar expectations and outcomes in their lives. And being able to recognize these general types is useful when offering spiritual guidance.

There is an entire system in Habad Hasidism dealing with the varieties of *nefesh ha'behami'it*, the 'animal soul,' and the varieties

---

[5] See Martin Buber, *Two Types of Faith* (1951).

of *nefesh ha'elohit,* the 'divine soul.' Among animal souls, some are like goats, sheep or oxen. The sheep is docile and gives you milk, flesh and wool, and that's good; but you won't get any work out of them. A goat, on the other hand, will give you the same; but they're *not* docile, and they tend to eat up your trees and everything else you don't want them to eat. Out of the ox, of course, you can get a lot work, pulling the plow during the harvest; but you have to watch out for the horns! And if you can deal with the bullishness, you can accomplish a lot. So a Habad Rebbe might speak about this person as a "goat," or that person as an "ox."

I remember, my papa, of blessed memory, used to say to me, "So and so is a Hannukah *lichtl,*" a Hannukah candle. This is good, right? "No," he said, "he just likes to shine; but you can't get any use of him. I prefer a *shammes.*" Do you understand? The goat is a like a Hannukah candle. You can't get from the goat what you can get from the sheep or the ox, at least not easily. So a Hasid talking about a 'goat' personality—often after taking a little Schnapps—would say, "Send him for *Azazel!*" Send him off into the desert, into the wild!

But, you know what? That's not entirely bad. *Azazel* means 'who God strengthens.' There is strength there and strengthening, and sometimes one comes out of the desert transformed.

The question is always—How to deploy the people with whom you are dealing? And that requires a conscious knowledge of their type and their individual uniqueness. Moreover, things that are easy to handle for one personality type, one that is more robust, may not be easy to handle for a personality type that is more refined. Furthermore, there are some people who have 'immune systems' that are robust, and others who have systems that are easily impacted by negative

Third Talk: The Rebbe and Spiritual Typologies

things. That also has to be considered when prescribing and giving people spiritual direction.

Personally, I cannot say that I am always doing this in an analytical and conscious way when I am working with people. Often, it is a lot more in the preparation, when I go into the heart and intuition space, into the right brain when preparing for *yehidut*, becoming aware without necessarily analyzing and grouping people.

But today, there are numerous instruments available for discerning introversion and extroversion, or whether one is a feeling, sensate, intuitive or thinking type—the basic categories we get from the psychotherapist Carl Jung, and which have gone into the Myers-Briggs test.

In the past, I have sometimes had groups I was teaching form circles, lining themselves up according to their birth dates, and therefore, their signs in the Zodiac as well. With a circle like this, moving from January 1st to December 31st, you get a circle of remarkable harmony, with everyone in their right place, and everyone having good overlap with their neighbor in terms of communication: Leos talking to Leos; Virgos talking to Virgos; and the end of the Leo spectrum standing next to the beginning of the Virgo spectrum, with that kind of overlap as well.

This is what I believe Bala'am saw when he looked at Israel dwelling in tribes around the sanctuary (Num. 24:2), each one representing a sign of the Zodiac: Judah (Aries), Issachar (Taurus), Zebulon (Gemini), Reuben (Cancer), Simeon (Leo), Gad (Virgo), Ephraim (Libra), Manasseh (Scorpio), Benjamin (Sagittarius), Dan (Capricorn), Asher (Aquarius), Naftali (Pisces).[6]

---

[6] These are the correspondences according to the Sefardic kabbalist and astrologer, Z'ev ben Shimon Halevi, who puts Levi in the center.

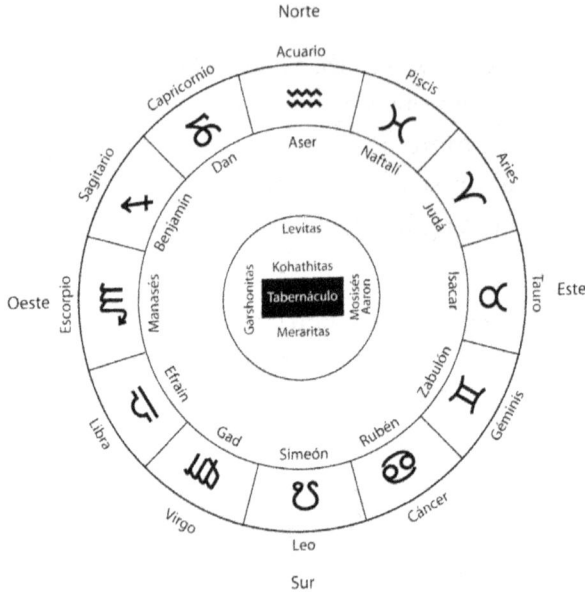

Z'ev ben Shimon Halevi, *Introduccion al Mundo de la Kabbalah*. Used with permission.

Imagine you are standing on one side of the circle, and opposite you, on the other side of the circle, a half a year apart from you, is a person of a very different type. You probably aren't going to find a lot of harmony with this person, because they will have a radically different viewpoint; but the likelihood is that you will find a good teammate there, someone who can do what you cannot. So they will oppose you sometimes . . . So what? The benefit of getting someone who is oppositional to you is that you will survive longer as a team. This is something important to keep in mind. While we like to be with *like* people, to have people who are *unlike* us is of great help to us, because they see the world differently and have different truths. For instance, I am a Leo born in August, and my wife, Eve, is an Aquarian born in February. Because of this, she sees the counter truth to my truth. And while discussion is not always easy, it is definitely worthwhile.

So an understanding of the Zodiac, and of where a person falls in its circle, is useful information to know when dealing with spiritual guidance and the communication issues that sometimes arise.

The House of Hillel
& The House of Shammai

Now, Reb Levi Yitzhak of Berditchev tells us that there are souls from the side of *hesed*, like Hillel, and souls from the side of *gevurah*, like Shammai. What works for one kind of soul doesn't necessarily work for the other, and this also has to be borne in mind in the counseling session.

Allow me to quote the passage from his *Kedushat Levi* in full, as it is one of the most audacious teachings I know of in Hasidism:

> Why do the Rabbis promise that all questions will be answered by Eliyahu ha-Navi when he comes to announce the *Mashiah* and not by Moshe himself, who will be resurrected at that time?
>
> Moshe died and we cannot hope to be helped in our current problems by Moshe, peace be upon him, who completed his life.
>
> Since that time, the Torah has been placed in our hands, and if one's soul is from the side of grace *(hesed)*, everything is pure, permitted, and kosher, and if it is from the side of rigor *(gevurah)*, the opposite holds true. Yet each person according to their own rung is

a vehicle for the word of the living God. This is why the Sages, realizing the need for grace in this world, set the *halakhah* (law) down according to the teachings of Hillel, for this is according to the world's need.

Now, one who is alive in this world is aware of the needs of the time and the attributes we need to live by. But one who is not alive on this plane does not know the attributes we need to live by in this world. Since Eliyahu is yet existing and alive, never having tasted the taste of death, remaining connected to this plane, he is suited like no other to resolve our doubts."[7]

This teaching is so important for us today, because it makes it clear that we need to be taught according to *our* needs. As Reb Levi Yitzhak says—Why don't we look to Moses for answers to our questions? Because Moses died to this plane of reality in *his* time, while Elijah did not, having ascended to Heaven while yet living. And being still alive, knowing our needs today, he can provide us with answers for *our* time. That is to say, Moses' personal answers do not reach beyond his own 'event horizon,' his own death.

Let me give you a little Hasidic anecdote about the Rebbe's event horizon:

A man comes to see Reb Elimelekh of Lizhensk and asks him, "Rebbe, is my new business venture going to be a success?"

Reb Elimelekh replies, "Wonderful! You're going to do very well," and he gives him a blessing.

On his way home from Lizhensk, the man stops to visit the

---

[7] Zalman Schachter-Shalomi and Netanel Miles-Yépez, *A Merciful God: Stories and Teachings of the Holy Rebbe, Levi Yitzhak of Berditchev* (2010), 77-81.

Third Talk: The Rebbe and Spiritual Typologies

disciple of Reb Elimelekh, the Seer of Lublin, who is known for his farsightedness. He asks him the same question. And the Lubliner says, "I'm afraid it's not going to be good for you; I can't give you a blessing, because I see it's not going to work out."

So now the man is troubled. After all, the master said it was going to be good; but his disciple says it's going to be bad. To whom should he listen? In the end, he reasons that the master must know better and he goes through with the business venture.

And, indeed, he was very successful... for a while. Then the business collapsed and he was wiped out. In the meantime, Reb Elimelekh had passed on, so the man went back to the Seer of Lublin to find out what had happened.

The Seer of Lublin said to him: "My master looked and saw your success, which occurred within his lifetime. But what he could not see was your failure, which was to happen after his passing. Since your failure was still to occur within my own lifetime, I was able to see it, and withheld my blessing."

This too is a very essential teaching, because types also create *event horizons* that sometimes a person cannot see beyond. That is why Rebbes are thought of as *neshamot klaliyot,* 'general souls,' who can understand many different types of people, and therefore, are not limited by a particular typological event horizon.

But, getting back to the teaching of Reb Levi Yitzhak, we see that our holy teacher, Hillel, comes from the side of *ḥesed,* 'grace' and 'loving-kindness,' while our holy teacher, Shammai, comes from the side of *gevurah,* 'discipline' and 'rigor.' So when Hillel gives advice, his *shoresh ha'neshamah,* the 'root of his soul,' is connected to a place of kindness and he speaks in a more understanding way. But when Shammai speaks, there is more severity because the 'root of his soul' is connected to a place of rigor. "This is why the Sages," according to the teaching of Reb Levi Yitzhak, "realizing the need for grace in this world, set the *halakhah* (law) down according to the teachings of Hillel, for this is according to the world's need." Likewise, this is the more understanding approach we must generally take in spiritual guidance, leaving room for uniqueness of the individual and the particular difficulties they might face.

Hasidic Styles: HaBaD, HaGaT, NeHY

There are people who are 'generalizers,' and people who are 'specializers.' If you ask the specializers to generalize, often they cannot do it. "Just give it to me in a couple of sentences," you say, and they have to unpack the whole thing for you with all the particulars. On the other hand, if you ask a generalizer to specialize, they often have trouble as well. "Give me some particulars," you say, and they can't tell you anything useful that will help you understand any better. As teachers, it is useful to be able to do both. But we must also be able to work with these different ways of apprehending.

Now, I was trained in the Habad Hasidic tradition, and HaBaD is an acronym for *Hokhmah, Binah, Da'at,* or 'wisdom,' 'understanding' and 'knowledge,' the upper triad of divine attributes on the kabbalistic Tree of Life. It is called HaBaD because the combination of these attributes defined the early development of this lineage. It was like saying, "We are into the intellectual attributes of Divinity." And HaBaD Hasidim often distinguished themselves from other Hasidim, whom they called HaGaT, an acronym for *Hesed, Gevurah, Tiferet,* or

Third Talk: The Rebbe and Spiritual Typologies

'loving-kindness,' 'rigor' and 'beauty,' the middle triad of divine attributes on the kabbalistic Tree of Life which primarily had to do with emotion. For HaGaT Hasidim, emotion was the way to serve God.

I really began to understand this when I started to visit the Bobover Rebbe, Rabbi Shlomo Halberstam. At the Bobover gatherings, there was a lot of emotion, a lot of joy. HaBaD was much more sober and serious by comparison. And when you would listen to the Bobover Rebbe's Torah, it was always Torah grounded in *hesed, gevurah* and *tiferet*. For example, here are a couple of teachings I heard from him:

"A *tzaddik*, a righteous person, is said to be 'good' and to receive the reward for the good that is done and the reward for the fruit of these actions as well. That is to say, a *tzaddik* gets the capital, the interest, and the compound interest. However, one who does evil receives punishment only for the evil, and not for the fruit of their actions also.

"Why should this be? If a *tzaddik* gives a dollar to someone in need, it is not just the exchange of a dollar from one person to another, but that dollar is also intended for help and for benefit, to get food, to meet the needs of a family, and for various other good things. However, the thief who steals a dollar, usually means to steal a dollar only to gratify their own needs. So the one who gives good receives the reward for the many good intentions also, while the one who intends evil is punished only for that evil."

You see, it isn't a teaching for the brain; it is a teaching for the heart. The Bobover Rebbe was a master of these kinds of teachings. Once, on *Shabbat Shuvah*, I heard him tell a wonderful story. He said, "People always think that they have to do a very heavy repentance *(t'shuvah)* for the sins they've committed. It's not so." Then he went on to tell the following story:

"There was long ago a kingdom in which the first still was invented, and everybody there started to drink Schnapps. Although the economy of the kingdom was based on agriculture, people almost immediately forgot about their animals and their farms. They only drank Schnapps. They used all the grain they produced to make Schnapps. Soon, hardly anyone was working because everyone was drunk, and this created a famine.

"When the king heard about this, he said: 'This is terrible. I won't permit it! The heaviest punishments must be dealt out for making and drinking Schnapps—lashes for offenders and death for repeaters!'

"The laws are decreed and they have no effect. So the king decides to go down and visit one of these farms. He enters the house of the farmer and sees he is under the table, drunk. A bottle sits on top the table! He shakes the farmer and says, 'Don't you know about the terrible punishments I've decreed?'

"The farmer says: 'Your majesty, you sit in the palace while we are all here grubbing on the soil. It's not so easy for us, so we take a drink.'

"The king says, 'You know I have to punish you, don't you?'

" 'Yes,' said the farmer.

"But the king thought—*If I'm gonna' punish him, I'd better know more about his crime.* So he tastes the Schnapps and immediately starts to cough and spit. Then he says, 'Drinking this is punishment enough!'

In the same way, God tastes our sin and says, ' *Feh!*' And thinks it is punishment enough."

Third Talk: The Rebbe and Spiritual Typologies

Do you see what it does to your heart to hear such Torah? It comes from such a view of the universe that sees these things in this wonderful, virtuous reality.

So that's HaGaT Hasidism. Later, I came to see that there was also what I call NeHY Hasidism, an acronym for *Netzah, Hod, Yesod,* or 'victory,' 'glory' and 'foundation,' the lower triad of divine attributes on the kabbalistic Tree of Life which primarily have to do with action. For NeHY Hasidim, everything is focused on action and activity—*mitzvah* campaigns and outreach.

Bratzlav Hasidism is in a special category, which I tend to think of as KaHaB, an acronym for *Keter, Hokhmah, Binah.*[8] And though Reb Ahrele Roth did much in the way of creating "consciousness commandments" for his Hasidim, some of his advice to his disciples for *davvenen,* or 'prayer,' is thoroughly rooted in the final divine attribute of *malkhut,* telling them to exert themselves in their bodies, like an ox carrying a yoke, like a donkey carrying a load. You don't have to derive anything from it, he says. If the king hires you to chop wood, you just chop wood. You should be glad that the king has seen fit to hire you! When you come into the *shul* of the Roth Hasidim and you see them *davvenen* like powerful oxen pulling the plow, and you see the bodily exertion that they put into their bodies, you can understand how it gets them somewhere!

It might not get *you* there, but it gets them there. And that's the thing to understand—for whom is this approach best suited?

---

[8] See Schachter-Shalomi and Miles-Yépez, *A Hidden Light: Stories and Teachings of Early HaBaD and Bratzlav Hasidism* (2011), 18.

Question and Answer Session

Question: When you were talking about Hillel, you said, "this is the more understanding approach we must generally take in spiritual guidance." Are there exceptions then?

Reb Zalman: Well, I once wrote an article called "The Dialogical Mentality" in which I talk about the regular theologian and the dialectical theologian.[9] The regular theologian would say that Hillel and Shammai are irreconcilable; but the dialectical theologian would say, *Eilu v'eilu divrei Elohim ḥayyim,* "Both are speaking the words of the living God." (Eruvin 13b) The idea is that, in the future, when the Messiah comes and all is as it should be, people will be able to do according to stricter way of Shammai. But until then, we must go with the more lenient ways of Hillel, who has compassion for the difficulties of our lives.

Shammai, you see, was like a Rinzai Zen master. When the man asks him to teach him the Torah that can be learned while standing on one foot, Shammai whacks him with a stick. Afterward, the man comes to Hillel, still smarting from his encounter with Shammai, and asks the same question. Hillel says to him, "Don't do something to someone else that you wouldn't want done to you . . . The rest is interpretation." (Shabbat 31a) And the man gets it. But if he hadn't gotten the whack from Shammai, he wouldn't have gotten Hillel's teaching in the same way. It takes both to create the proper understanding.

Now take this case that was brought before both Hillel and Shammai. Two men go in together on buying a slave. Later, one of them gives the slave manumission. So, is he still a slave?

[9] Zalman Schachter-Shalomi, *Paradigm Shift* (1993), 13-15.

Third Talk: The Rebbe and Spiritual Typologies

Is he free? Or is he both a slave and a free man? Hillel says, "Three days he is free to work for himself; three days for his remaining master; and on the *Shabbat* he rests." But Shammai says to Hillel: "You took good care of his master, but this poor guy still has a dilemma: he can't marry a slave woman because he is part free; and he can't marry a free woman because of the part that is still a slave. You have to force his remaining master to give him manumission also. Later on, if he can, the former slave will have to pay him back. But to keep a person in this impossible situation isn't right."

This is one of the cases in which we follow the decision of Shammai instead of Hillel. When you are dealing with such a difficult problem, you have to bring the messianic mind-set of Shammai to this case. You just can't leave someone in this kind of paralyzing situation. You have to help them out right now. We can't wait until the Messiah comes for some things to be straightened out in the world; we have to act 'messianically' right now.

This is one of the contributions Reb Arthur Waskow has made with his interpretation of *Hilkhata lim'sheha*, the law that brings us the Messiah. He says, "If we want the Messiah to come, we have to live as if the Messiah has already come."

So there are clearly times when the more rigorous attitude of Shammai is necessary, when we have to say, "This is how it has to be."

Fourth Talk

The Rebbe's Assessment of the Hasid's Spiritual Situation

THANK YOU FOR RISING . . . Please be seated.

Once, after I had done something that had particularly pleased my Rebbe, the sixth Lubavitcher Rebbe, I came into his office as he was sitting at his desk and he made an effort as if to rise for me! I was completely floored by the gesture, as I knew it was extremely hard for him to move, owing to his paralysis, and I had not seen him do anything like this before. My feeling is that this was the day on which I really got my *s'mikhah*, my 'ordination.'

Scales of Moral and Faith Development

There are two scales of moral and faith development I have found very useful over the years, and absolutely necessary if you are going to help people in counseling and spiritual direction. One is the Kohlberg Scale, and the other is the Fowler Scale.

The psychologist Lawrence Kohlberg, who taught at Harvard University, carried out some important experiments with one of his graduate students, Moshe Blatt, which seemed to verify how one moves from one level of moral development to the next. In simple form, the Kohlberg Stages of Moral

Development look like this:

Level 1 (Pre-Conventional):

1. Obedience and Punishment Orientation:

How can I avoid punishment?

2. Self-Interest Orientation:

What is in it for me?

Level 2 (Conventional):

3. Interpersonal Accord and Conformity:

Social norms, and the good boy/girl attitude.

4. Authority/Social-Order Orientation:

Law and order morality.

Level 3 (Post-Conventional):

5. Social Contract Orientation

6. Universal Ethical Principles:

Principled conscience.

Interestingly enough, the RaMBaM—Maimonides—makes nearly the same case in his commentary on the Mishnah (Tractate Sanhedrin) when he talks about different levels of motivation for observance. Basically, he says: "We first say to a child, '*Read*, and I'll give you candy.' Then we say, '*Read*, and you'll be the best in the class and get *koved*, respect.' And then we say, '*Read*, and you'll find it interesting and entertaining.' Then, '*Read*, and you'll become an outstanding scholar.' '*Read*, and then you'll be able to help the community.' Finally, you get to the point where you'll say, '*Read*, so you'll know Torah.' " You get to intrinsic motivation from extrinsic motivation. It's

Fourth Talk: The Rebbe's Assessment

very similar to Kohlberg's scale of moral development.

Now, if you give advice to a person and you don't know on what scale of moral development they are, you can prescribe something that will not be *sam ha'ḥayyim,* 'life-saving medicine,' but *sam ha'mavet,* 'deadly poison' for them. Instead of helping them, you may actually set them back. So, you've got to find out how a person views a given situation so you know how to prescribe for them.

Kohlberg shows us that a person who is, let's say, within the Conventional category of moral development, at stage 3, for instance, and you try and tell them about a Post-Conventional morality, at stage 5 or 6, they won't know what you're talking about. It will sound totally absurd to them. But if a person at stage 3 is introduced to an idea of morality from stage 4, they are able to understand it!

So assessment of a person's stage of moral development is important for spiritual guidance. For, once you know it, you can introduce them to the stage immediately above it. That will create the stretch that is necessary for growth, and keep them from becoming complacent. And every once in a while, you should ask yourself, "Where do I belong on this scale?"

Now, the other scale of which you should be aware is Fowler's Stages of Faith Development. James W. Fowler, a professor of theology and a Methodist minister, drawing on Jean Piaget and Lawrence Kohlberg's work, came up with the following stages:

Stage 0 (Primal or Undifferentiated Faith):

> *Birth to 2 years, characterized by early experiences of comfort, safety and security vs. discomfort, neglect and abuse.*

Stage 1 (Intuitive-Projective Faith):

Three to seven, characterized by the psyche's unprotected exposure to the Unconscious.

Stage 2 (Mythic-Literal Faith):

Mostly school children, characterized by a strong belief in the justice and reciprocity of the universe; deities are almost always anthropomorphic.

Stage 3 (Synthetic-Conventional Faith):

Adolescence to adulthood, characterized by conformity to religious authority and the development of a personal identity. Conflicts with one's beliefs are ignored due to a threatening fear of inconsistencies.

Stage 4 (Individuative-Reflective Faith):

Usually mid-twenties to late thirties, characterized by angst and struggle. The individual takes personal responsibility for his or her beliefs and feelings. As one reflects on one's beliefs, there is an openness to new complexity, but this also increases the awareness of current conflicts.

Stage 5 (Conjunctive Faith):

Associated with mid-life crisis, acknowledging paradox and transcendence conveying the reality behind the symbols of inherited systems. The individual resolves the conflicts of previous stages with a complex understanding of a multi-dimensional, interdependent 'truth' that cannot be explained by any particular reason.

Fourth Talk: The Rebbe's Assessment

Stage 6 (Universalizing Faith):

Characterized by treating others with love, compassion and justice in recognition of their shared membership in a universal community.

If you get into a discussion of something like theodicy—"If God is good, how can bad things happen?"—how you can deal with it will depend on the level of faith development of those with whom you are discussing it. If you try to answer a person on a level of faith development that is well beyond their own, they won't get it. Tell a little child, "Yea, though He slay me, yet will I trust in Him." (Job 13:15) How can you say that to a child when you want to make sure that he or she will be entrained with good sensible habits? It belongs to an altogether different level of faith development. A child's understanding has to be expanded slowly.

Reb Shneur Zalman of Liadi, in his *"Ḥinnukh Kattan,"* quotes Proverbs, *Ḥannokh lana'ar 'al pi dar'ko*, "Teach the children according to their way, so that when they get older, they will not move from it." (22:6) But Reb Shneur Zalman says: Come on, should they be stuck all their life on that childish level? No, that's not the meaning of the verse. It means, teach them in such a way that it will expand with them as they grow older, so that they have no need to leave it behind.

The psychologist Gordon Allport spoke of something he called "functional autonomy of motives." He said, Freud always had you looking for the origin of a behavior, going back to the very beginning to find out why you do something. But Allport says, we don't do things as adults—even the same thing—for the same reasons we did them as children. We have different motivations now.

Likewise, if we look at the *ta'amei ha'mitzvot*, the 'reasons for the commandments,' understanding why they were given and what they mean, we will see that there has also been a kind of functional autonomy of motives. First, we are told, "God will be angry if you do it differently." Or, "We don't do that because the Canaanites did that." Then, a little later, there is Midrash, and after a while, Kabbalah to explain why we *really* do the *mitzvot* and what they mean. The Italian kabbalist, Menachem Recanati wrote an amazing book on *ta'amei ha'mitzvot* based on the Zohar. So, you see, as you grow, your motives also become more sophisticated and more spiritual.

Endo-Skeletons and Exo-Skeletons

There are varieties of life on this planet that are endo-skeletal, having skeletons on the inside, and varieties that are exo-skeletal, having skeletons on the outside, like insects and crustaceans. An exo-skeleton doesn't allow you to grow much, whereas, an endo-skeleton supports growth.

The Hebrew, *etzem,* means 'bone,' and *atzmut*, means 'essence.' You see the relationship? We need a strong spine on the inside, to know something essential in us to support our growth. This is why I am always trying to teach about the 'deep structures.' If you want to make a change in the liturgy, you need to know something about its deep structure. If you don't understand that, then you don't know how to make an intelligent or a holistic change. Understanding of possibilities and real freedom come from an understanding of 'bone' and 'essence,' *etzem* and *atzmut*.

Some people are afraid of change, holding to a kind of 'floodgate theory'—"If you change one thing, everything is going to fall apart!" But that's mostly true for exo-skeletal beings; vertebrates can make more changes, and need to.

Going back to the levels of faith, we say to children: "You have to have faith in me; I'm your father," or "your mother." It sounds strange, but later on, you can transfer that faith to other things. You can say: "Look, you now see that I am flawed; I make mistakes." And from there, you transfer faith to a social body, or the tradition. We keep transferring and raising the faith to higher and higher levels, finally placing it in both the strongest and most risky of places—*God*.

The inner testimony of God's reality cannot be taken from us, but we cannot prove it either. Only at the highest or deepest level of faith development can we say, "Yea, though He slay me, yet will I trust in Him." (Job 13:15) Or still better, as the tradition says of Jacob, "You have promised to be with him in the fire and in the water." (Isa. 43:2) It doesn't say, "God will rescue him from the fire and the water," but God will be with him in the burning and the drowning. This is an altogether different level of faith.

Knowing Your Audience: A Lesson

I want tell you a couple of stories from my own life that taught me important things about how to work with people. You know, there is a lot to be said for 'knowing your audience,' knowing with whom you are dealing as a spiritual leader.

I want to tell you a story from a time in my life when I failed to do so as a congregational rabbi in the 1950s. Today, I look at it as an object lesson on how *not* to go about introducing new ideas.

In 1953, I was offered a rabbinical post at Ahavath Achim, a small Orthodox congregation in New Bedford, Massachusetts.

The Geologist of the Soul

The *shul* was supported by the children and grandchildren of its regular *minyan*, so that "*zeide* should have a place to go and hang out." And those parents and grandparents were mostly people who wanted everything in the *shul* to be like it was in Shtockelshtock, the small town in Lithuania from which most of them had come.

So I come along and start asking them, "So how was it in Shtockelshtock? How was the rabbi in Shtockelshtock?"

"Eh," they'd answer, "he was a greedy guy. He would always travel around *kalendeven* to pick up his income. He wasn't available for much."

They would ask me, "Why don't you *davven* like the *ḥazzan* in Shtockelshtock?" So I would ask them about the *ḥazzan* in Shtockelshtock.

"Oh," they'd say, "neither a voice, nor an ear. And he didn't understand *p'shat*." But, I should do it like they did it in Shtockelshtock!

One Rosh Hashanah, maybe my fourth in New Bedford, I was coming up with my sermons and said to myself, "I'm going to talk about this business of Shtockelshtock and where we need to change." So, not long after, I gave a sermon about how positive changes could be introduced. "It doesn't have to be like it was in Shtockelshtock," I said, "but we also want to be careful not to throw the baby out with the bath water. So we want to move carefully in making those changes."

Then, on Yom Kippur, I give another sermon about repairing wrongs and talk to the congregation about how they were always looking for fights with the Conservatives. And since there was a lot of talk about the H-Bomb at the time, I said how much more energy could be gotten from fusion (bringing

Fourth Talk: The Rebbe's Assessment

atoms together) than from fission (splitting atoms). So why don't we concentrate on getting along, rather than fighting with each other, because there is unlimited energy in fusion.

After the holiday, a couple of guys are talking in the *shul*, downstairs below my office, where I can hear their conversation. One guy says to the other, "What did the rabbi have to say this year for Rosh Hashanah?"

The other answers, "You know, he said something like this . . . 'The atom bomb fell on Shtockelshtock because they threw out the baby with the bath water.' "

I tell you, at that moment, I lost all my taste for giving sermons.

There was another Friday night when I decided to liven things up and do some experimenting. Just as Picasso had his "Blue period," at that time, I was in my "Protestant period." I was a member of the Ministerial Organization in New Bedford and I even had my own radio program. For my intro music, I would play George Beverly Shea's—the Reverend Billy Graham's *'hazzan'*—"He Watches Over Israel." During that period, I was attending different types of Protestant Christian services to see how they did things, and by then had been to Baptist services and attended a number of Quaker "Friends Meetings."

Inspired by what I had seen, I decided to do something entirely different one Friday night. I told the *shammes*, the synagogue attendant, not to distribute the prayer-books that evening, saying, "We won't need them." The *hazzan* and I had an introit at that time. We began singing *"Shalom Aleikhim"* and *"Lekhah Dodi"* as we walked into the *shul* and did a few things by heart. Then I invited the people to do something different. I say: "The Talmud says, 'The early Hasidim would sit for an hour in silence before prayer.' (B'rakhot 5:1) So I suggest that we sit for about twenty minutes in silence, and if something comes up for you, something you would like to share, you can get up and share it." Of course, this is what was done in the Quaker meetings I had attended.

Twenty minutes passed and it was perfectly quiet. No one was getting up to share anything. Finally, a *shul* member who was a refugee from Germany rose and said: "Are we not like a Camera obscura, hermetically sealed by organs and senses. If we could only make a little pin-hole in that enclosed box, not only would the light come in, but the beautiful picture from beyond would also be reflected within." Amazing! An insight very much like what was written in the Talmud, *Pitḥu li petaḥ k'ḥuddo shel maḥat*, "Open a hole the size of a needle, and God will open a hole the size of palace." (Midrash on Shir Ha'Shirim 5:2)

That was great, so I say: "We so rarely get to pray for what we really want in our service. So I would invite you to take the opportunity to do it now. I'm not asking you to pray out loud, but when you finish your personal prayer, I'll open the *aron kodesh*"—which holds the Torah—"you can come up, and we'll all pray for your intention. 'Whatever Charlie needs, God, please give it to him. And let us say, Amen.'" And they actually did it!

Then I asked the people to come up and count their blessings. I say: "We get up in the morning and say the *Modeh Ani* in gratitude for being given another day. It's so beautiful. But how often do we really count our blessings? For this, you don't even need any preparation. You can just say, 'I'm grateful for this . . . I'm grateful for that.'" So whole families came up to the ark and counted their blessings and shared with people what blessings they had been given. Finally, the president of

Fourth Talk: The Rebbe's Assessment

the synagogue, a young lawyer, came up and said, "I thank you God for having such a rabbi."

I was on top of the world. It was a great success!

The next Thursday, I got a special delivery letter, which read: "We have 423 prayer-books, and they're meant to be used! — The Board of Directors."

I'll tell you something . . . it was my own fault. I didn't prepare them beforehand. I didn't say anything to anybody about what I was going to do, or why, and I got into trouble for it.

A little later, the board was having a meeting and I asked to attend so that I could find out how I was doing. Somehow, they got it into their heads that I was going to ask them for a raise. So they sent me out from the meeting, and for about three hours they talked and came up with a fifteen-item list of complaints! When they read them to me, I was bemused to find that number seven was, "Not modern enough," and number eight was, "Too much English." I laughed . . . It was the last time I laughed in New Bedford.

Sometime before, there had been a man in who came to me looking for help with saying Kaddish for his father who had passed. I went to his house, helped him with his *t'fillin*, taught him to do *ma'ariv* first, and later on to do a *minḥah*, and later a *shaḥarit*. Eventually, he joined the *shul*, became a member of a committee, then a member of the board, and finally president of the *shul*. And it was he who convinced the board not to renew my contract.

It was a painful lesson, and something to remember: we cannot simply impose things on others.

The First Assignment

I had actually done far better a few years earlier; and this story, I suppose, tells you how I eventually came to be in the position I am today.

Back in 1949, when my friend, Rabbi Shlomo Carlebach and I were still in our twenties, I was a congregational rabbi in Fall River, Massachusetts, and he had gotten a job as a rabbi in New Jersey. He had also started a small group that he called, "Taste and See that God is Good!" which met in his father's synagogue. Once, when I was in New York, he had me come and celebrate with them. It was a creative time for us both—I was secretly reading about other religions, translating *hasidut* into English and writing English lyrics to Hasidic *niggunim* on the accordion, while, at the same time, Reb Shlomo was playing the piano and beginning to compose his own beautiful *niggunim* and singing them with his group of students.

That same year, we attended a celebration in New York on the 19th of Kislev in December—a Lubavitcher holiday—in the Rebbe's house. Because the Rebbe, Reb Yosef Yitzhak was ill at the time, only a few people were being admitted to the *farbrengen*, to the 'gathering.' Indeed, because he couldn't have a lot of people around him, the *farbrengen* was being held in what used to be the bedroom of his mother, just off the end of a corridor. So most of us just stood outside of the door singing *niggunim* and waiting for an opportunity to say *"L'hayyim!"* to the Rebbe.

From time to time, the door opened and one of the Rebbe's men would come out and admit someone as others went out. After some waiting and singing, Reb Berel Haskind comes to the door, looking like 'Hop-a-long Hasidy'— his black hat tilted in a cowboy-ish turn and bottles of Schnapps sticking

Fourth Talk: The Rebbe's Assessment

out of his belt, his *gartel*, like a couple of six-shooters on either side—and he points at Reb Shlomo and I and waves us in!

We enter the room, and the Rebbe says, "Take *l'hayyim.*" Reb Berel Haskind came over and poured us some Schnapps, and the Rebbe says, *"L'hayyim!"* and we drink it down. Then, the Rebbe continued, *K'dahy ihr zolt onheyben foren tzu colleges,* "It is time for you to start visiting the colleges." He suggested we start with Brandeis, and offered us a little bottle of Schnapps that was sitting on his table to take along with us. That was it!

Reb Shlomo and I left very excited. But, the Rebbe hadn't told us what to do. So we decided to start on Hannukah and make a tour of the Boston colleges (because I lived in Massachusetts), starting with Brandeis, and going on to Boston University and the others.

A few days later, I went to Providence, Rhode Island on the train to pick Shlomo up and we started on this jaunt. *Oy!* We felt very much like emissaries of the Ba'al Shem Tov! I had brought with me my accordion, some copies of translations of *hasidut* I had made, and a big reel-to-reel tape player on which I had recorded some Hasidic *niggunim* with a Hammond organ. I was also carrying thirteen pair of *t'fillin* I had refurbished to give out to people who would promise to wear them.

It was snowing when we arrived, and we had to *shlep* the accordion, tape reorder, *t'fillin,* and boxes of papers all the way up the slippery steps going up to "the Castle" at Brandeis. We enter the campus cafeteria where a "Hannukah dance" was in progress, and see that all the lights are out except for a spotlight someone is moving around and shining on the couples dancing to the music of the juke-box. We step inside with our black hats, heavy beards—in those days, beards weren't that common—and *tzitzit* hanging out, and the spotlight lands right on us, the strangest couple there! Everyone stopped and looked at us. I swear, even the juke-box gave a shiver.

We found a table and put out the translations and the tape recorder, and before long, people started to meander over. First, they listened to the music, and then they started to ask questions, which sent Shlomo into a fit of storytelling and people crowded around to hear him. While Shlomo talks, someone says, "That sounds like Hindu mysticism." So, I know that is my customer, and I pull him aside, saying, "Have you read the *Upanishads?* Have you read the *Bhagavad Gita?*" Then I would say, "Well, take a look, we also have that in Hasidism!"

So, a second circle formed that wanted to hear about mysticism and philosophy, and I was showing the Hasidic translations to people. Then someone wants to know, "What does Hasidism have to say about evolution?"

I say, "Evolution? Who knows it better?" and I explain the evolution of the 'Four Worlds' of spiritual consciousness descending from the heights of *Atzilut* on down to the world of manifestation in *Assiyah*. It was wonderful! We began singing *niggunim* well on into the night, and everybody got into it.

At two o'clock in the morning, after distributing the *t'fillin,* we packed up and began descending the icy steps from the building, when someone yelled after us, "Hey, there's another way that isn't so icy; you're gonna break your necks!" For whatever reason, we didn't listen and continued down the steps until we reached the bottom unscathed. Some kids, who had seen our easy descent, decided to follow and ended up on their backsides. Someone asked, "How'd you manage to get down without falling?" Without missing a beat, Reb Shlomo piped in with a grin, "If you hold on to *Above,* you don't fall

Fourth Talk: The Rebbe's Assessment

from a *Below!*" And, poof! We went out with a bit of magic and great one-liner!

We knew we had made an auspicious start in our mission for the Rebbe when the university president warned us never to come back! Taking our cue from early Hasidism, opposition was the measure of our success. That was the beginning for us in the work that would become central to the rest of our lives.

But, you see, this was our audience, and even within it, there was a type of person who wanted to hear the different kinds of things each of us had to teach. Reb Shlomo had his set of customers and I had mine.

The first students who came to me had good Jewish backgrounds, familiarity with all the basics, and some had even been to *yeshiva*. But they were also dissatisfied with the Judaism they had known and were looking for something better. Often they had already been exposed to wider horizons in other religions and felt that they could talk about both with me. And this was an important connection for us both.

The American *Pashuteh Yidden*

Who is the audience today? Another short story:

Sometime in the 1940s, a brilliant young American student in his twenties, fresh from reading Martin Buber, came to see professor Abraham Joshua Heschel, the scion of numerous great Hasidic lineages who had decided not to follow in his father's footsteps. He knocks on Heschel's door and says, "Sir, I'd like to become a Hasidic Rebbe."

Now, here is a corn-fed American—brought up in a relatively unobservant or secular Reform Jewish household, a student of philosophy and religion, inspired by the example of Hasidic piety in Martin Buber's writings—talking to Hasidic royalty—born in Eastern Europe in the lap of Hasidic learning to be a Rebbe, who chose to become a professor instead—about becoming a Hasidic Rebbe! Can you appreciate the irony of it, and the distance to be overcome?

But this is precisely where we are today. There are more and more people like this young man, inspired by Hasidism and Kabbalah, who want to align themselves with those deeper teachings of Judaism, and who want to live in the "virtuous reality" seen in the stories of Hasidism. The inspiration is genuine; but more often than not, they don't know much Hebrew, don't know much about *halakhah* or even Judaism in general. They are the *pashuteh Yidden*, the 'simple Jews' of America!

The Ba'al Shem Tov was continually singing the praises of the *pashuteh Yid*, the 'simple Jew,' and *emunah pashuteh*, 'simple faith.' In his time, he was talking about those Jews who were often working so hard to scrape out a living, in such trying circumstances, that few of them had any chance to receive an education or learn anything of depth about Judaism. Nevertheless, they were deeply pious and prayed and did what *mitzvot* they knew with such sincerity and simple purpose that the Ba'al Shem Tov counted their prayers as more significant than those of the learned elite and made them a model for his learned students.

The *pashuteh Yid* of today isn't necessarily poor or uneducated; indeed, the opposite is often true! How many *pashuteh Yidden* do I know with advanced degrees in business, the arts, physics or philosophy? It's not about intelligence or wealth; it's about a purity of heart and a simple desire to grow in piety and closeness to God. But some of the old issues for *pashuteh Yidden* remain; in our world, as in theirs, there is so little time to invest in spirituality after making a living and meeting the needs of our families. There isn't a lot of time left to learn Talmud and Torah in depth, so they go to get the best inspirational material available, they try to pick up whatever *kabbalah* and *ḥasidut* they can, and learn to pray and meditate as deeply as possible, within the time allowed.

The *pashuteh Yid* of today, like the *pashuteh Yid* of the past, isn't concerned with looking smart or appearing pious; their concerns are simple, direct and sincere. The *pashuteh Yid* says: "What is God asking me to do in this moment? Whatever it is, I want to do it. I want to walk my talk, to live according to God's will. I want to make my home holy. I want to be hospitable to others. If you need a *gemillat ḥesed*, a favor, help of some kind, a loan or donation, I want to be there for you." There is a genuine warmth there. The *pashuteh Yid* is more interested reading Martin Buber's *Tales of the Hasidim* than his erudite and philosophical *Origin and Meaning of Hasidism*.

Necessary Outreach

People have often come to me with gratitude, saying: "I used to have to keep my Judaism and my Yoga, or my Zen Buddhism, in two separate places. Now I've found that I can keep them in the same place, and I'm so grateful." But there are still so many people out there who are involved in trying to make peace between competing interests, who feel like they are constantly betraying one part of themselves while serving another.

I don't yet have the sense that we have done enough to reach these people, to make room for them, and to show them how to create a more holistic relationship between their Judaism and their other commitments. I feel that we don't do enough active outreach. If someone new comes into a service or a celebration, we don't welcome them and shake their hand, or show them when we are to rise and when to turn the page, they often feel very intimidated and out of place, and don't want to come back. So, a helpful hand is important.

We have so much to offer for which people are hungry; but they don't know we exist. So we need to do more work in the world to make what we are doing available to them.

Question and Answer Session

Question: Is the function of a Rebbe like that of a psychiatrist? Can a Rebbe take the place of a psychiatrist?

Reb Zalman: When a psychiatrist speaks to a patient, the person is often, in a manner of speaking, an object of study. Though interested in curing the patient and helping them adjust to life, the approach is to derive not only a healthy being, but an accumulation of information about human beings for his future knowledge.

A Rebbe gives him or herself over completely to the person. When seeking a solution, the Rebbe does not study the person who has come for help, but is more emotionally involved with them. Only a small part of a Rebbe's work is like that of a psychiatrist's. That is not the Rebbe's primary function.

Yet, when one needs aspirin for a headache, the Rebbe will tell the person to go to the drugstore and buy some, and not try to substitute the prescription with something else. If the person needs a psychiatrist to cure their ailment, the Rebbe

Fourth Talk: The Rebbe's Assessment

will not try to substitute his or her own cure.

Question: As a rabbi, I sometimes feel I was not adequately trained for what I would encounter in an actual congregation; was this your experience as well?

Reb Zalman: I remember an occasion in New Bedford when the *shammes* came to me and said, "Rabbi, the Fourth of July is on *Shabbat* this year; where should we *davven,* upstairs or downstairs?"

Now, in those days, the upstairs was the bigger part of the *shul* and was used for big services, while downstairs was a little *beit midrash* used for small services. "Should we *davven* upstairs or downstairs?" Well, I had just come out of Lubavitch, full of enthusiasm, and thought: *Fantastic! On the Fourth of July, nobody has to go to work! We'll have a packed house!* So I said, "Upstairs!"

He said, "Rabbi, are you sure?"

I said, "Yes, because nobody has to go to work; there'll be a fuller *shul.*"

He looked at me with eyebrows raised and said, "You'll be happy if you have a *minyan.*" And he was right.

There needs to be a course in our seminaries on the 'realities on the ground.'

Question: What is one of the biggest differences between the *pashuteh Yidden* of yesterday and the *pashuteh Yidden* of today?

Reb Zalman: If the *pashuteh Yid* of old were to come to one of our homes today to celebrate *Shabbat,* what would they find? How many people are singing *z'mirot* at the table or telling stories of Rebbes? Which family sits and reads on *Shabbat,* or spends time talking together? The television is on, the computer is in the lap, and the phone is in the hand, and we are sitting and eating in front of them.

The *tish,* the 'table' of *Shabbat,* is the greatest invitation into *Shabbat.* If we let it go, we lose one of the most important aspects of *Shabbat,* and we lose what it can do for us. I believe people are actually hungry for it; but the habits of today are strong. It will take a strong effort by the *pashuteh Yidden* of today to re-institute the *Shabbat* table in our families, and the *Shabbat* atmosphere in our homes; but it may save us from the disconnectedness happening all around us. And in doing it, it is important to allow it to be seen, to model this *pashuteh* behavior for others.

You also need to have *havrusot,* study partnerships, to keep the lateral connections and learning traditions of Judaism alive. If you don't learn together, you may not develop in the right way.

People who begin to learn Torah later in life have the blessing of not having their learning contaminated by the things some people were taught as children. So you can hear the words of Torah from an altogether higher level.

Question: You've talked about a lot of positive qualities regarding the *pashuteh Yidden,* but it seems to me, there are also a lot things that need help too, especially around ignorance of the tradition. Is that not the case?

Reb Zalman: One day, I actually thought it was a joke when someone called me and said, "Rabbi, is it true that on *Shabbat* you don't have to sit *shiv'ah?* So it's okay for us to go to the

Fourth Talk: The Rebbe's Assessment

store then?" Clearly, there is an educational gap to overcome with some people; but we want to be careful not to bury enthusiasm and an individual's unique approach as we educate. The education needs to be tailored to that person's unique needs.

Question: Earlier you mentioned theodicy; can you talk about how you usually handle these issues of God and good and evil?

Reb Zalman: This is a very difficult topic and requires a lot of explanation. And, as I said, usually has to be tailored to a person's needs.

In Kabbalah, in the world of *Atzilut*, of being, there is no evil; because there is only unity, wholeness, and all of it is seen as good.

In the world of *B'riyah*, thinking, it is still mostly good. Imagine, a physicist comes up with a brilliant theory and everybody says, "Wow! That sounds fantastic!" Because the reality-testing of the theory is still ahead. You might have a couple of unanswered questions; but, all in all, it sounds pretty good. The shadow costs increase as we descend through the worlds. When planners propose a highway to get you from Kingston to Ellenville, it sounds wonderful. But by the time it actually comes to building it, the real costs show up. Every mile of highway costs a life—car accidents, deer and other animals killed by cars, *et cetera*.

In *Yetzirah*, the world of feeling, it seems like the evil and good are in just about equal measure. This is where the drama takes place, all the melodrama—the 'good guys' and 'bad guys.' And, if I want to tell the story of the drama, I say: *"Oy!*

Nebukh! I'm such a victim; do you know what that bad guy did to me?" It's all in the language of feeling and drama.

In the world of *Assiyah*, action, it seems like there is more evil than good. Here is where the actual action takes place, where the physical being is actually ailing. So that's the perspective in the Four Worlds.

Once, the Reverend Matthew Fox and I had this conversation about duality and non-duality. We were saying, if you want to project evil on someone else, and say it doesn't come from God, you have to create this basic duality, with God and good on one side and Satan and evil on the other. But if you want to say there is no dualism, no God and Satan duality, then you have to pay the penalty and make room for evil in God. In other words, if God is only good, God isn't all-powerful. If God is all-powerful, God isn't good.

Rebbe Nahman of Bratzlav proposed an emerging vision of God, a 'growing God,' when he proposed a different explanation of "Abraham knew You from youth." He says, most people read it as "from Abraham's youth." But Rebbe Nahman says it should be read, "Abraham knew You from when You were a young God."

There is the Godhead which is infinite, and the God which is the interface between us, the finite, and the infinite Godhead. That God is often a mask, a *partzuf,* a root metaphor that we ourselves project.

Imagine I have a moment in which I experience the infinite as a kind, nurturing, good, progenitor begetting me. So, I naturally associate it and call it by name "Father" or "Mother." Or, if I have a sense of being fully known and scrutinized, as if I am standing before the bar of justice, I will naturally think of God as "Judge."

Fourth Talk: The Rebbe's Assessment

There is a remarkable movie called *Defending Your Life*. In it, you have a person who died in an automobile accident and comes to the other side of life, which looks like the Denver International Airport, with escalators going up and down, and trams taking people from place to place. Finally, he has to defend the way he has lived his life. And it's not easy, because the accusing attorney can say, "Let's look at such and such a date and see the video of exactly what you did." You can't escape the camera! It's the judge.

There is a wonderful story that is passed around by Zen Buddhists, Taoists and Sufis. A man has an only son who falls off a horse and breaks his leg. Now he is lame and people say, *"Oy! Nebukh!* That's terrible." The man says, "We'll see." Then the recruiters of a warlord come into town and take all the young men but his son. And people say, "Oh, that's so wonderful! So good!" But the man only says, "We'll see." And each time there is an event that comes and turns the meaning around, re-contextualizes things. So who are we to know what is good and bad? All that is left is total surrender, to say, "I don't know."

So we come up with these root metaphors and project them to the infinite . . . It's nice, but it can also become an idol and cause us lots of trouble, lots of disappointment, like the Great and Powerful Oz in *The Wizard of Oz*, or the god-figure in *Star Trek V: The Final Frontier*.

Each time we say the *Sh'ma'*, we invest in the Jewish godness in that archetype, in that root metaphor, in that *partzuf*. And amazingly, at a certain moment, that *partzuf* begins to live for us. It begins to shimmer as if *Ain Sof*, the Infinite, has put it on as a garment . . . *Ain Sof* is wearing it! And through it, something begins to shine. But the reality toward which we are really praying is behind the root metaphor.

Fifth Talk

The Rebbe's Compassion and Prayer-work

I WANT TO READ YOU PORTIONS of a letter that was written to me some time ago. I receive many such letters from people who want to talk to someone with a 'higher ceiling' than they can normally find. Often they have had unusual experiences and don't have anyone with whom they can talk about them:

> I guess I should describe to you what I have been experiencing. It seems unusual to do in a letter to someone I don't really know, but my sense of you is that you would probably understand and probably not think I'm crazy. [. . .]
>
> By the time we got to the *Lekhah Dodi*, the singing was filling the room and I felt it was also filling my soul. When I closed my eyes to say the *Sh'ma'*, I had a sort of vision of Rabbi Akiva at the time of his death. It was as if I had a glimpse of where his soul was at that time and what it would be like to be so completely focused on the love of God that being tortured to death seemed immaterial. It put me in a different spiritual state than I had ever been in and it lasted all night. But I assumed that this was probably a one-time experience and that it would fade. Then, the next morning, when we davvened the *Kedushah*, the *Shaharit Amidah*, I felt as if my soul was trying to rise upward out of my body. It was as if my soul was in two places at once, within me

and above me, rising toward heaven, looking down on all of us davvening. I was moved, but I was also afraid. Some piece of me was saying, "What if my soul doesn't know the way back to my body? Who would come and bring me back?" Still, I knew in the back of my mind that I was supposed to be involved with the service, so I dragged my soul back into myself, but I was a little disoriented. [. . .]

So I told someone, my teacher. He was supportive. He said he was an academic scholar of Kabbalah and not a *moreh derekh* ['teacher of the way'] and that I need to find one. He suggested I contact you, as have several others since. [. . .]

Since then, I've had many other experiences, as if the heavens have opened and are staying open. Some of them have been experiences of descent, like the one *Shabbat* morning.

Once, when I was davvening, we were davvening in the woods, my friend said that she could feel that I had "gone," though I was standing right next to her. Sometimes, a word, a phrase would jump out at me and I davvened with a new meaning and image after. Sometimes, it felt as if all the words were jumping out at me—word after word, phrase after phrase, image after image, meaning after meaning. It was as if the words of prayer came alive and sometimes, while standing outside, the colors looked brighter, as if I'd never seen those colors before. [. . .]

Putting on *t'fillin*, I felt as if I was being electrocuted. It wasn't a physical sensation; it was if there were a charge running between the *shel rosh* and the *shel yad*.

Fifth Talk: The Rebbe's Compassion and Prayer-Work

And I had a fear it might overwhelm me and short-circuit my mind."

This is a person who needs guidance from a deeply grounded and spiritually experienced teacher. Just as the academic professor of Kabbalah, to whom he originally talked, referred him on to someone with more practical experience, so must you if you do not have a more integrated understanding of such experiences.

One does not function as a Rebbe without having done the work on a number of different levels, and without forming an integral map for oneself. A Rebbe has to push the envelope of spiritual experience and find a way to operate in different dimensions of consciousness. Only then can one find a way to offer the appropriate guidance to a person having these kinds of experiences.

That is not to say that you have to have experiences like this person was having. I once had a conversation with Gregory Baum, a German-born Catholic theologian, and asked him, "Do you do spiritual direction with people?" He looked at me like 'What are you asking me for?'

I said, "I'm interested in the work of spiritual direction."

So he tells me that he is working with somebody who works in a factory and is sometimes overtaken by divine raptures while at work on the machines! Sometimes, he says, the guy has to bang his hands against the machines to get himself grounded enough to stay present. Then he said to me, "I sometimes envy the person with whom I am doing spiritual direction; I wish I had those experiences myself."

This is often the case with us; but it is not necessary to have these same experiences. What is necessary is to have your own relationship with God and to explore the spiritual terrain thoroughly yourself and to offer what you can to a person in need. However, if you are out of your depth, you must be responsible enough to recognize it.

But as I have discussed issues of counseling and spiritual direction at length in my books, *Spiritual Intimacy* and *Sparks of Light,* I'd like to move on to a discussion of the kind of compassion we need to have for the people we are serving, and of intercessory prayer.

The Great Compassion

What is *raḥamim rabbim,* the 'great compassion'? In Buddhism, they speak of the *bodhisattva* as one who is just a short step away from freeing him or herself from the round of death and rebirth, but who stays in the game out of compassion for others, to help liberate them. Just one step more and they could be re-absorbed in what the Zohar calls, *l'ishta'ava b'gufa d'malka,* to be totally 'drawn into the very body of the King,' no longer separate within that Totality. The drop is re-absorbed back into the ocean and merges with *Ain Sof,* the Infinite. The longing for this can be very great; but when the *bodhisattva* or *tzaddik* looks around and sees how much people are suffering, he or she says, "No matter how many incarnations it takes, no matter how much trouble it causes me, I won't take that way out until I have helped to liberate each and every one of them."

Imagine you are a soul about to incarnate, about to enter a child. At that moment, you get a vision of the whole life you will lead: the colic of the newborn; the taunting of other children; the shame of bed-wetting; failures in school; disappointments in love; the responsibilities of being the firstborn, or being the second, always running behind; a whole life of ups and downs, work and dark places; and finally, decline and death. And now you have a chance to back off or dive into life. What will you do? The likelihood is that soul will still recognize what a precious opportunity it is to live in a body, with all its discoveries and consciousness; and, in spite of all the pain and difficulties, with great love and compassion, will say yes and undertake the experience of labor and birth in order to take that journey!

Now, imagine the moment before the Big Bang, and every pain, every oppression and every death that ever shall be is felt within God. It is to that place, and from that place in us, that we make the appeal that we're going to make in prayer. It is not a place of pity or sentiment; it's too vast for that. It holds the all, but holds and pours out a *rahamim rabbim*, a 'great mercy.' It is the field being held behind all of creation. That's the field we want to reach in prayer.

The Efficacy of Prayer

I would like talk a little about the efficacy of prayer. Are we just making ourselves feel better with prayer? Or does it actually effect a change somewhere?

Years ago, I read about the Reverend Franklin Loehr in *Reader's Digest* and I contacted him. He had done this wonderful experiment to see if prayer makes a difference. He put some seeds in two identical boxes—box A and box B—under identical conditions, to see if there would be a measurable difference in the plants he prayed over. And there was!

Later, I met Richard Castel, an emissary of the Hopis, at a Rainbow Meeting in Oregon. He told me that the Hopis are supposed to be like the Hasidim of Native Americans. He also said that when he first turned to the Hopi ways, he learned how they originally planted corn. They take a planting stick and drive it into the ground. Now, Arizona is a pretty arid place, and you have to go fairly deep to find any moisture. So you have to drive that stick in the ground until the tip finds a little moisture, and that is where you plant the seed. Then you use the stick to measure to the next place in the row and make another hole in the same way. At every hole in which a seed is planted, you offer a prayer. And this is how the whole field is planted!

But the modern Hopis Castel was working with no longer did things this way and were annoyed that he wanted to plant using this "old-fashioned" method. So they told him to start at the other end of the field and not to get into their way. He did, and of course, they were able to plant their part of the field a lot faster. But when the harvest came in, his corn, planted with prayer according to the old method, was about a foot taller, and the ears of corn were richer and healthier!

In Dr. Larry Dossey's prayer experiments, he found that prayer was definitely effective, but that it was more effective to pray with a "Thy will be done" attitude than for a specific healing. So, some people are exploring these things, and it should at least give you some confidence about the potential efficacy of prayer.

Investment in the Outcome

Once, I asked my Rebbe, Rabbi Menachem Mendel Schneerson, about interceding for people in prayer. He told me, among other things, "Don't forget to put some money into the *pushke*," into the 'charity box.' Having a *pushke* available to you

Fifth Talk: The Rebbe's Compassion and Prayer-Work

when you're praying for another person is really important, even if it's only 18 cents that you give. It's a way of saying, "I'm invested."

Here's a story I heard from Rabbi Shlomo Halberstam, the Bobover Rebbe:

Reb Yitzhak Eisik, the Kalever Rebbe, had a son, Meir, who was not what most people expected him to be. He hung out at the inn and played cards and did things that the Kalever Hasidim thought unfit for the son of a Rebbe. So they talked to him about it, saying, "It's an affront to your father's memory to have you doing such things . . ." But it didn't help. Then they decided to go to his father's grave and recite *T'hillim*, to recite Psalms and fast until a change happened in the son.

On the third day of psalm recitation and fasting, Meir didn't go to hang out with his friends at the inn. So his friends came to his house and said, "What's the matter with you?" He said, "My father came to me in a dream and said I can't do this anymore." His friends said, "Foolish dreams! Forget it!" Before long, he was back in the inn playing with them. But the Kalever Hasidim continued to pray and fast.

The next day, he didn't go to hang out with his friends at the inn. Again, the friends came to his house, and by noon, they had coaxed him out to play cards. Still, the Hasidim fasted and prayed.

The next day, he broke his leg! His friends asked him what had happened. He said, "My father came to me in my dream and said again, 'If you don't want to listen, I'll have to make you listen.' Then he picked up the little stove there, smashed it on my leg. So I'm not coming out with you anymore." His friends left him behind and ceased trying to engage him. But the Hasidim came to his house to visit him and to help him heal. And that's how they brought him back.

Hasidim also came to the Bobover Rebbe, Reb Shlomo the First of Bobov, pleading for help with the son of Reb Zalke, of blessed memory (a major disciple of the Seer of Lublin), who wasn't behaving so well. "Rebbe, what should we do?" He responded: "If you're prepared to do what the Kalever Hasidim did, then we'll be able to do something. If you're not prepared to do it, then we won't." That is to say, if you care enough, then you are willing to do something, and to give something. Dedicating some money to *tzedakah*, 'charity,' is one way of doing that.

Freedom, Determinism, and Curling

Sometimes people raise the question of 'freedom or determinism' around intercessory prayer. That is to say, whether we can effect change or not through prayer because God may already have predetermined events. And if they are *not* entirely predetermined, then how much freedom do we have? And should we use it? There are a number of ways to answer these questions. One of my favorite answers comes from the Hasidic tradition and goes like this:

> Someone asked Reb Pinhas of Koretz, "How can we pray for someone else to repent when that prayer, if granted, would curtail another person's freedom of choice? Is it not said by the Rabbis that 'everything is in Heaven's hands, except the fear of Heaven?'" (Megillah 25a; B'rakhot 33b)
>
> The Koretzer answered, "What is God? — *The totality of souls*. Whatever exists in the whole can also be found in the part. Therefore, in any one soul, all souls are

Fifth Talk: The Rebbe's Compassion and Prayer-Work

contained. If I turn in *t'shuvah*, in 'repentance,' I already contain in me the friends whom I wish to help; and, likewise, they contain me in them. My *t'shuvah* makes both the *them-in-me* better, and the *me-in-them* better. In this way, it is easier for the *them-in-them* to become better as well.[10]

So the question is, do our prayers for change in others steal freedom of choice from them? But Reb Pinhas' answer turns the whole enterprise of praying for others on its head. We are all connected, he says, and it is better to do our prayer-work and make the necessary repairs from that perspective.

That's one way of looking at the situation; but it doesn't really answer the question of whether we actually have freedom of choice, or whether everything is already determined in our world. This situation really only became clear to me when I was on a canoeing trip on the Lackawaxen River, a tributary of the Delaware River, in Pennsylvania.

Usually, when we think of freedom of choice, we think of life as if it were Lake Placid, on which you can steer your boat in whatever direction you want to steer without difficulty. Determinism in life, on the other hand, is like going over Niagara Falls in a barrel; there's nothing you can do. But, most of the time, life is actually like canoeing on the Lackawaxen River, or white-water rafting down the Colorado River. The river is pulling you along—often pretty fast—but if you see a boulder coming up, you have some power to steer. I can't wish the boulder away, but I can learn to read the river and react accordingly.

---

[10] Zalman Schachter-Shalomi and Netanel Miles-Yépez, *A Heart Afire: Stories and Teachings of Early Hasidic Masters* (2009), 142.

Likewise, with those things we pray for, there are some rare occasions when things are totally unobstructed or completely blocked, but most of the time, there is a little room to maneuver.

Another *mashal* or 'analogy' I like comes from the Scottish and Canadian sport of curling. In curling, one player takes a big rounded stone with a handle on it and slides it forcefully down a lane of ice while two "sweepers" use brooms in front of it to influence the trajectory of the stone by creating a layer of moisture under it.

In the same way, our *karma* is very much like the initial "delivery" of the stone. Its velocity and basic direction is not subject to much influence, but a good team of "sweepers" can steer it a little by creating a shallow channel in front of it. My sense is that this is what we can achieve in most cases with intercessory prayer when a set of karmic conditions is already in effect. We can create a shallow channel to steer the *karma* in a more congenial direction.

Though sometimes, the work we need to do is as simple as an attitude shift.

Taking Hold of God's Willingness

Bishop Phillips Brooks once said, "Prayer is not overcoming God's reluctance; it is taking hold of God's willingness."[11] If that "willingness" exists, how do we take hold of it? What do we need to do? A story I heard from my friend, Reb Shlomo Carlebach, to illustrate:

Reb Yitzhak Eisik of Zydichov was one of the great disciples of the Seer of Lublin, whose custom it was to spend some

---

[11] This is also attributed to Martin Luther.

Fifth Talk: The Rebbe's Compassion and Prayer-Work

time alone in prayer in his upper chamber each day, during which he was not to be disturbed. But a time came when one of his grandchildren was sick, and the illness had progressed to the point where the doctors were saying: "This is a crisis. If nothing changes, the child will die."

Now everyone was afraid to disturb Reb Yitzhak Eisik's prayer, but his grandchild's life was at stake. So they decided to send another of his grandchildren, whom he loved, with the message: "Now is the time to pray, or else Yankele might . . ." But the grandchild they had sent was a true heir of his grandfather and decided to alter the message somewhat. He went upstairs and knocked on the door of his grandfather's upper chamber and said: '*Zaide, Zaide,* Yankele is almost well . . . Just a little more prayer on your part and he'll be all better!"

So Reb Yitzhak Eisik prayed just a little more to complete his grandson's healing and amazingly, the crisis abated and, before long, he was completely healed! Later, when the Rebbe came down and heard the story of what had really happened, he called the grandson who had given him the message and said: *Hast's seikhel, wirst sein a Rebbe.* "You know how to use your head; you'll be a Rebbe!"

Why did it work? Because the attitude was not of "overcoming God's reluctance, but taking hold of God's willingness." Believing that God was favoring the child's recovery and, experiencing joy and enthusiasm around that, the Rebbe was able to envision the child's healing clearly, and to confidently put the seal on it. And this change of attitude made all the difference.

We have to recognize just how important a contribution we make, and how our attitude affects the outcome.

Once, a delegation of townspeople came to see the Apter

Rav, Avraham Yehoshua Heschel of Apt, asking him to fast with them and to pray for rain. The fast day had been proclaimed and they had come to fetch him. But when they arrived, they found him eating chicken! "Rebbe!" they cried, "Why are you eating?"

The Apter Rav answered, "What do you think you are showing God? That you can live without food? Better to show Him that you need to eat!"

They took his point, but said, "Won't you at least come out with us to pray for rain?"

"No," he answered. "You're not serious. Not a single one of you has brought an umbrella along!"

Creating a Will in God

The Maggid of Mezritch used a *mashal,* an 'analogy' that went like this. "Imagine there is a father who loves his child"—the Maggid had a son he loved and used this image often—"and this father is invited by his child to play horsey. So papa gets down on the floor and allows the child to ride around on him like a horse, when in comes a colleague who says, 'What are you doing on the floor? A scholar like you!'"

The father replies, "But the child wants it!"

The colleague says, "So what? He should get everything he wants?"

Then the father says, "You don't understand; when I saw how much he wanted it, I wanted it too!"

In other words, the desire of the child created a willingness in the father. In the same way, the Maggid tells us, our own desires, born of delight and good will, create a willingness in

God for those same things. And that's what *y'hi ratzon*, 'may it be your will' is all about.

Question and Answer Session

Question: Do you think there are more people having extraordinary experiences today—like the ones mentioned in the letter you read—than there were in the past? And how should they be dealt with?

Reb Zalman: Years ago, Itzhak Ben-Tov, who wrote *Stalking the Wild Pendulum*—and who died in an airplane accident when his DC10 crashed over Chicago—talked about the emerging consciousness, and how some people who were experiencing breakthroughs back then were being put in mental institutions by a society that was not yet ready to handle it. And yet, this is precisely what our planet is trying to foster, the next level of growth of consciousness. So keep that in mind and treat such experiences that are brought to you with the care that you might offer a newborn.

Question: You cautioned us about giving advice beyond our knowledge; could you say a little more about that?

Reb Zalman: The problem is, you start talking to protect your ego, talking beyond your understanding, and you can set a person back or do some damage to them. A similar thing happens with intuition. There are moments when intuition is talking and it suddenly comes to an end, and we feel somewhat awkward and try to continue; but it is usually done and you should really pause. But when things are beyond your understanding, or out of your arena, do your best for them in the moment and refer them on.

Another situation of this sort occurs when you don't want to be vulnerable to a particular spiritual issue in a certain moment and start to talk—pardon my language—bullshit. This poisons the relationship with the person who has come to you with an open heart, honestly looking for answers and for help. In Hebrew, the phrase is, "Pushing them away with a straw." You're putting them off; you just don't want to deal with what they're bringing to you.

Question: When multiple people come for counseling, how do you hold your intention from one person to the next?

Reb Zalman: The fourth Lubavitcher Rebbe, Reb Shmuel of Lubavitch, thought the bigger problem was to clean out the mind-filter between counseling sessions. Otherwise, you end up giving advice for the last person you saw to the next person! I remember a therapist who would answer the telephone and do all kinds of things in the 5-10 minutes before a session (sessions being 50 minutes). I always thought, *Man, when are you going to do your recycling?* You need that time to clear out the filter and get ready for a completely different person. You don't need to junk it up with more mind-clutter.

Sixth Talk

The Rebbe's Tool-box for Intercession

Blessed are the ones who do not give up, even when the 'door' is stuck. One more try and it yields. It just doesn't pay to give up.

I WANT TO GO INTO THE WORK of intercession now, because a lot of what is required of people who are in positions of spiritual leadership has to do with intercessory prayer. People will come to you with prayer requests, saying, "Please pray for this person" or "Pray for me," and you need to take that seriously, and know how to do that in an effective way.

Untying Our Tangles

In his teaching about Tu B'Shvat, the great Sefardic rabbi, Yosef Hayyim of Baghdad, offers an alternative form of the *Ana b'Koah*, 'we beg you' prayer, attributed to Rabbi Nehunia ben HaKanah. If you look in different prayer-books, you will see that the *Ana b'Koah* is said on Friday evening before *Lekhah Dodi*. It is also said at the deathbed. It's the kind of prayer that you say when you need something powerful to accompany your request. So, on those occasions, you make an *Ana b'Koah*. I would suggest you learn it by heart for those occasions.

I usually translate the first line of it into English as, "Source of mercy, with loving strength, untie our tangles." Whenever I am out driving and I hear a siren—a fire engine, a police car, or an ambulance—I say a quick *Ana b'Koaḥ* that they get there on time, and that everything should be okay. It's a good prayer for all occasions, and an important prayer for intercession. Here is one English translation of it done more conceptually with one of my students:

> We beg You!
> With the greatness
> Of Your right hand,
> Untangle our
> Knotted negativity.
>
> Accept our prayer—
> Strengthen and purify us,
> God of Strength.
>
> The guardians
> Of Your Unity
> You protect like
> The pupil of Your eye;
> Bless them, *Tzaddik*,
> And always remember
> Their needs.
>
> Powerful and Holy,
> Your goodness
> Guides us ever;
> One and Unique,
> You turn to those
> Who regard You
> In holiness.

Sixth Talk: The Rebbe's Tool-Box for Intercession

> Please accept our plea
> And hear our cry,
> Knower of mysteries.[12]

But, as I was saying, there is also another version by Rabbi Yosef Hayyim of Baghdad which uses the same initials from the original lines of the *Ana b'Koah*. My translation of it into English reads like this:

> Oh, would that
> The beautiful Presence
> In endless compassion
> Shed Its Light so radiant!
>
> Oh, would that Your Will,
> God, most Exalted,
> In sound and
> Inflection encoded,
> Manifest in us!
>
> Oh, would that
> The mating (*zivvug*),
> Most complete and sacred,
> In infinite greatness,
> Attain to the crowning!
>
> We sprang
> From the Light-drop
> Of the womb of the *Tzaddik*
> To grow to completion.

---

[12] Translated with Netanel Miles-Yépez for the prayer-book of the Inayati-Maimuni Sufi-Hasidim.

We entreat in this prayer,
The hope of our people
That the blissful fulfillment
Send us its blessing.

Oh, would that the mating,
Most holy, most sacred,
Be roused to its peak-point,
As all power is sweetened!

May the root
Of the *Tzaddik*,
The way of the Sacred,
Find its completion
Right here and now!

   I don't need to tell you the Freudian implications of the "root of the *Tzaddik*" and "The way of the Sacred." But, do you see how the language is used in a sacred context and filled with holy purpose? The suggestion is to recite this as an invocation before the 'sacred union.'

   One of the Hasidic masters, Reb Mikheleh of Zlotchov, in his *hanhagot*, prescriptions for spiritual practice, also suggested to his Hasidim that they should give *tzedakah* after making love. So this is another instance in which the *pushke*, the charity box comes into play, except here it is used in gratitude for the enjoyment of that sharing, adding that energy to the offering. Can you understand how this gives a lift to "giving bread to the hungry and bringing the homeless into the house" (Isa. 58:7) and every other blessing you give with that charity?

Sixth Talk: The Rebbe's Tool-Box for Intercession

Charity, Simple Prayers
& The Use of the Mother's Name

There is a story in which Rebbe Nahman of Bratzlav is sick, and he tells his grandson, "Pray for your *zeide* to get better." And the child says, "If you give me your watch, I'll pray for you." The Hasidim laugh and say, *Shoin gevor'n a Rebbe!* "He already knows how to take [an offering] like a Rebbe!" But Rebbe Nahman takes out his watch and gives it to his grandson who closes his eyes and says, *"Ribbono shel 'Olam, zeide* is sick. You can make him better; so please make him better. Amen." The Hasidim say "Amen," and then laugh again. But Rebbe Nahman says, "What are you laughing at? What do you think I do when I pray for you? Walk with my boots up to heaven?"

These stories show you that you shouldn't price yourself out of the market. Often, a simple prayer and a little *tzedakah* are exactly what is called for in a situation. In the Jewish tradition, we ask for the name of the person and the name of their mother, as it says in the Psalms: *Ani avdekha ben amatekha; pitaḥ ta l'mosserai,* "I am your servant, the son of your maidservant; open those things that close me in." (Ps. 116:16) It is really important to say, "I am praying for your servant, the son of your maidservant," to use their names if you know them.

Rebbe Nahman was asked why we use the mother's name in prayer and the father's name for calling a person to the Torah reading. First, he says, *Derekh tzaḥot,* "In the way of wit." This is what someone says before making a holy joke. Then he says, "When you pray, you've got to start with a sure thing. With the mother, *you're sure."* Then he says, "But more seriously, there's always an 'indictment' *(kitrug)* involved when someone is sick. Something is not right there. In order to handle that 'indictment,' you always have recourse to this argument:

'*Ribbono shel 'Olam*, maybe this person isn't such a good person; but for nine months his mother carried him under her heart, and then gave birth to him with labor; for that alone, you should help!'"

Enlisting a Prayer Partner

Before his passing, the holy Ba'al Shem Tov asked his disciples to sing the *niggun* of Reb Mikheleh of Zlotchov, which he had named, "The Melody that Stirs and Invites Divine Mercy." And when they finished that, he said to them, *Ich bin mavti'ach l'dorotechem*, "I promise you, for generations to come, whenever someone sings this *niggun* with the great arousal, seeking mercy with a longing to be harmonized with God's will, no matter where I am, I will hear it and sing along and pray with you." My Rebbe, Rabbi Yosef Yitzhak of Lubavitch, when he told this story commented, "There are some angels who bring intelligence to souls."

Once, when I was a very young man, I was *davvenen* with a group of Rebbes and their Hasidim vacationing in one of the kosher hotels in the Catskills, getting deep into longing, when a Galicianer Rebbe turned to me and said, *"Nu?* Young man, what have you got to say to us?" So I told this whole story of the Ba'al Shem Tov and the history of this *niggun* I had learned from my Rebbe. And when I had finished, he said "Wow! So sing us the *niggun!"* It was terrible ... I had forgotten it! *"Oy!"* he said, "You've got such a good gun and no bullets!" After that, I memorized it and made sure never to forget it. It's a *niggun* with real power, and one that can be used with a real purpose in prayer.

Likewise, when I want to bring the energy and wisdom of other Rebbes into my prayer or intercession, I often sing *niggunim* that are composed by them, or associated with them in some way. It is like enlisting a prayer partner and magnifying the effect of what you are doing.

Praying through the Worlds

Now, how do you go about praying for another's needs? As I mentioned earlier, Reb Shneur Zalman of Liadi taught, "You have to see that person's *neshamah*, or 'soul,' in the light of *Adam Kadmon*, the original template."

How does one do that? One way is to ascend the ladder through the *Arba Olamot*, the 'Four Worlds.' It is not easy to fix the problem on the level where it seems to exist, so we have to get 'above' it to do the fixing. Often there is so much shadow in the world of *Assiyah*, the world of action, that we can't do the work there. We have to go to a higher level. People who do mediation work know that you can't solve the conflict at the level of the conflict; you have to raise the dialogue to a higher level where the two parties can find common ground and some agreement.

Start with *Adam Kadmon*, seeing the person as their *neshamah*, their soul stood in its original light, in that divine splendor. Then, begin to bring something down for that person from that place, down through the *Arba Olamot*, the 'Four Worlds.'

In *Atzilut*, the world of being, it is easy, because here is perfection which has just taken on a shape. In *B'riyah*, the world of thinking, you are looking at who the person is, and why they should be healed. You might say good things about them, be their advocate and make a case for them. Sometimes you really have to be a skillful lawyer here and find the loopholes to get your client off, as Reb Menachem Mendel, the Kotzker Rebbe did for his son-in-law.

The father of his son-in-law comes to the Kotzker Rebbe and says: *"My* son—*your* son-in-law—is deathly ill. He needs your prayer. He's such a *lamdan,* such a learned person, so pious, one of God's jewels!"

But the Kotzker answers, to the father's horror, "He's not so special . . . He's got a lot to learn yet."

Later, when the son-in-law was better, he asked his father if he had gone to the Kotzker Rebbe for prayer. The father doesn't know what to say; he's not sure he wants to tell him the terrible thing the Kotzker Rebbe had said about him. But the son insists. And when he hears what the Kotzker had said, he says, "Ah-h-h," and smiles. "You see, father, when I was so sick, it seemed that there was nothing left for me to do here. After all, I have learned so much Torah already and have been so acclaimed for my great knowledge that it looked like I was finished. So the Rebbe was forced to say to heaven, 'He's got a lot more to learn yet.' And that saved me!"

So sometimes you have to frame it in a special way to achieve the desired result.

Now, in *Yetzirah,* in the world of feeling, you have to arouse the heart, seeing that person in the light of love, in the utter perfection that God, at the very first thought of the person's existence, had in mind for them, and from there, draw down the thing you are praying for.

And when we return to *Assiyah,* the world of action, it is important to see the person as healed or well.

Sixth Talk: The Rebbe's Tool-Box for Intercession

Praying through the Tree of Life

At the same time, you can also use the *Eitz Hayyim*, the 'tree of life' and the lower seven *sefirot*, the 'divine attributes' as *tzinorot*, or 'pipelines' for the prayer.

This is where you need to use your *seikhel*—a combination of intelligence, wisdom and street smarts—to accomplish something in your prayer, just as we saw in the example with the Kotzker Rebbe.

Starting with *hesed*, or 'loving-kindness,' we might ask, "Why should I pray for this person?" Answer—"Because I care for them . . . I want them to get well . . . I wish them all the good."

But *gevurah*, or 'rigor,' is a check for that and requires some skillful work. Here is where judgment comes in. For example, maybe the person is sick because they haven't taken care of themselves . . . "Everybody warned them," says a voice in your head. To lead a person through this is subtle work; you must get to a place of lifting the *gevurah*, and saying, "From now on, they are going to shift and a change in their life."

Believing in the shift and making a commitment to it are really necessary. I remember when my Rebbe, Rabbi Menachem Mendel Schneerson, was asked about reincarnation and replied: "Sure, we believe in reincarnation; but only a fool waits to die before beginning their next incarnation!" That is why we change the name, or give an additional name to a person in times of serious illness. We're saying, "Yes, this person has a history associated with this old name; but the new name has different possibilities!"

In *tiferet*, or 'beauty,' after taking away the judgment, we hold the person in a place of sensitive and sensible compassion.

In *netzah*, or 'victory,' the prayer is that all the necessary helpers and help will begin to manifest, like finding the right person in the right setting, and that it is a day when that right person is having a good day and feeling sharp. Sometimes, we need to get everything in the right alignment.

I remember a situation like this from when I was still in the Lubavitcher *yeshiva*. On occasion, the Rebbetzin Nehama Dinah, the Rebbe's wife, would come down to the kitchen to taste the food the *yeshiva* boys were eating. It was her quality control. She wanted us to eat well, and for the food to taste good. And, in this way, she became friends with the cook.

Well, one day she noticed that her friend wasn't looking so good; she looked somewhat pale and wan and didn't seem to have much energy. So the Rebbetzin says to her, "From all over the world people come to see my husband to ask for blessings and for healing; and right here, under our own roof, the woman who cooks for our boys is sick and doesn't go to him for a blessing?" So she took her right upstairs to the Rebbe's office.

The Rebbe looked at her for a moment, gives her a blessing, and takes out some paper and writes a letter which he puts in an envelope and seals. "Take this to Dr. Bondi," a Viennese doctor who lived up in Frankfurt on the Hudson in Washington Heights.

So she made an appointment to see Dr. Bondi, but didn't give him the letter. He checked her out and couldn't find anything wrong. Then she gave him the letter. He read it and immediately sent her to the hospital for an X-ray. She then had an operation that saved her life!

To find the right alignment here, you might be silent and watch for the right instrumentality; maybe you'll get some guidance about where to send this person.

Then in *hod,* or 'glory,' we see the healing in the most elegant way that it can be seen. Sometimes, what holds a healing back is that it is not approached with the right etiquette, with the exact kind of care and beauty that a person needs. I remember how a guy named Joe August was putting beautiful paintings in hospital rooms and playing music and sounds from nature that would help aid the healing process.

Here we might also ask for a quick recovery.

In *yesod,* or 'foundation,' a kind of limbic, mammalian happiness needs to come into play, and we ask that their energy or *chi* should be replenished.

And finally, in *malkhut,* or 'sovereignty,' we might ask for a good outcome and visualize the person as well again.

Afterward, give some *tzedakah,* some 'charity,' as we discussed earlier. It is your investment in a good outcome.

Trouble-shooting in the Tree of Life

Sometimes we get hung up at one rung or another in the prayer-work and we have to find a way through it. For this, I recommend breathing into the space of the particular *sefirah* where you are stuck.

If you are stuck in *ḥesed,* breathe into the *ḥesed.* Take three or four breaths there and say, while exhaling audibly, "I want to move through." Likewise, you might breathe into *gevurah* and make it soft. Breathe into *tiferet* and make it large. Breathe into *netzaḥ* for empowerment. Breathe into *hod* for smoothness.

It is in *malkhut* that we often have a lot of trouble. Some of it is ego trouble. We want the healing or help to have a gift tag on it from us: "*Ribbono shel 'Olom,* when they get better, please make sure they know it was *my* prayer that did it!" Rescinding and letting go of that impulse is the last phase of the intercession.

Reb Naftali of Ropshitz would pray, "*Ribbono shel 'Olam*, you send me all these Hasidim, and I pray for them, and they do get better; but maybe could they get better without coming here?" You get the idea? He wants to pull his ego out of the equation.

The Ba'al Shem Tov once entered a *shul* and promptly turned around and walked out. "Why?" asked his disciples. "Because," he said, "It's full of prayers." "Isn't that good?" they asked. "No," he said, "They are prayers that haven't ascended." The place was constipated with prayers that wouldn't go up; the 'enter button' hadn't been pushed. Relinquishing the credit and attachment to the results is a way of doing that. After having prayed, we say, "Take this cup from me; thy will be done." That's like saying, "I leave this in your hands." As Larry Dossey points out in his report on his experiments, letting go of the result was a key feature in a prayer's effectiveness.

The Preparation, Suggestions & Context for Intercessory Prayer

What kind of prayer you do depends on your available time and setting:

1. If there is a traffic accident or some other emergency, it requires immediate prayer of whatever type you can manage to offer;

2. Use the *Ana b'Koaḥ* whenever you hear a fire truck or police siren, or whenever you're not in an expansive mid-space;

Sixth Talk: The Rebbe's Tool-Box for Intercession

3. With more time, you can go to Psalm 119 (an alphabetical arrangement, with 8 verses for each letter) and recite the verses corresponding to the letters of the person's name, asking for the specifics of their healing;

4. When you have the most time, pray through the Four Worlds and with the Tree of Life, as was described earlier.

When you are preparing to pray for someone you know, or who has requested your prayer:

1. Make an ablution, bathe or shower;

2. Meditate to come to a quiet space within;

3. Express your appreciation and love of that person to God (honor them within like the apple of your eye);

4. Remember to be a good and skillful advocate (as we saw in the story of the Kotzker Rebbe, who interceded for his son-in-law by saying that he hadn't yet achieved what he needed to achieve).

Pray together when you need to do so. When people don't know how to pray for themselves, sometimes you can do it together. You might ask the other person to pray with you "so that we can say '*Amen*' together." This loosens bindings on the heart.

Remember, you can also do an intercession for a group of people, just as you would for an individual. Instead of dealing with an individual soul, in this case, you are dealing with a 'soul-cluster,' as we discussed earlier.

You should have a daily practice of some type of intercessory prayer if possible. Often a problem is on-going and needs to be remembered in daily prayer for a while. It needn't be grand. Trying to make it so only leads to ego-inflation. Just be sure to touch-in with the need when you can. And keep praying as long as the soul is in the body.

If you remember, you might ask the *neshamah,* the soul of the particular person to join you in the prayer; also, qualify the prayer as being "for the highest good of this soul."

Sometimes, it might even be necessary to insist on what you're praying for; be the mouthpiece for that part of God's heart that wants a healing to happen!

And in the end, don't forget to give *tzedakah*, 'charity.' It was said of Rabbi Elazar, "He gives the poor a penny and prays." This is in fulfillment of the verse, "I, through charity, will see Your face." (Ps. 17:15) Sometimes I ask people to give time and not money. Time is the 'coin' in which the rich cannot give more and the poor cannot give less. It's all the same. We all share time, that thing that we have in common. So, if you want to donate time as a *mitzvah* for your prayer, that would also be good.

Experiment with Intercessory Prayer

Now I want to think of someone for whom you want to pray. Keep them in mind until you feel the prayer rising and then use one of the means I have discussed—simple prayers with their name and their mother's name, a *niggun* to bring along a prayer partner, praying the *Ana b'Koah*, or praying through the Four Worlds and the Tree of Life.

In your mind, imagine what it would *look* like, what it would

Sixth Talk: The Rebbe's Tool-Box for Intercession

feel like, what it would *be* like, if your prayer was answered, seeing the person you prayed for in the fulfillment of the prayer. *Ken y'hi ratzon,* 'may it be God's will,' *amen.* And when you're done, put some *tzedakah* in the *pushke*.

Question and Answer Session

Question: During the experiment with intercessory prayer, I found myself praying for my father, which surprised me, as I have been angry with him and am in an early stage of healing yet. But I found myself praying for his soul. There was no need for physical healing, nor an emotional crisis to be overcome; it was simply for his soul, as if I was fighting for it. Does praying for a person's soul make a difference in the prayer?

Reb Zalman: There is a kabbalistic statement which says, *Ein ha'dinin nimtakin ela' b'shorsham,* "Harsh decrees cannot be sweetened (shifted) unless you go to the root." Praying for a person's soul is going to the root.

Question: When I was in B'riyah, I saw so much about the life of the person I was praying for; but the thing is, I don't actually have a lot of biographical data about them. So I wonder, how much is my fabrication and how much is a genuine reflection of their life?

Reb Zalman: Quite naturally, we wonder: *Am I just fantasizing this, or is it real?* Well, I want to tell you, I once tried to get into my mother's place in life when she was eleven years old. And it was in some ways frightening to be her then. Thankfully, I had an occasion later on to check with her and see how much of it was just right on.

People who used to do the Silva Method, at the end of the process, were asked to diagnose someone to see if they could function like a medical intuitive. And it was amazing to see how often they were right on. My sense is that even if it isn't all 'factic,' you're quite possibly onto a truth.

Question: In my prayer, I was noticing the limits of what I can do and how not everything I thought of was helpful; have you ever had this experience?

Reb Zalman: Absolutely. Once I got this wonderful insight that we are like the white corpuscles being sent to places of infection. The white corpuscles go and die along with the infection. But I was praying for a child and I asked myself, "Are you willing that this child should be one of those white corpuscles?" That moment was very hard for me. And then I said, "Never mind *Ribbono shel 'Olam*, I thank you very much for the *midrash* of the white corpuscles, but you have other ways of doing it. Please heal this child."

When you notice your limitations, you have to say, "What I can contribute to this moment is the time and energy I put into my prayer." Also, "I cannot get into another person's life and take away their initiative for things they need to do. I can't do this; but at this moment, this is what I want to do. And, I feel that is what I'm called to do." So the *yetzer ha'ra'*, the 'evil inclination' that keeps coming up is you have to do more than is your call at that moment. But even that energy can be put into the *davvenen,* saying, "That which I cannot do, I put into the *davvenen.*"

Sixth Talk: The Rebbe's Tool-Box for Intercession

Sometimes our prayers can't ascend because we are holding the prayer too tightly. Sometimes we squeeze our hands together and have our eyes closed so tightly, saying, "Please, God, please!" that the prayer is not released from our tightly held bodies. This is largely done in the world of *Assiyah*.

Can you imagine what it would be like to go to the place where we love the person and feel the love for them, letting that love be in our hearts, holding it up before God instead?

If we begin to look at the life of that person in its fullness, the purpose of that being and what that being has already done, and the potential that being has, holding that up to the light, the good naturally increases. There is greater possibility.

In *Atzilut*, we can say: "*Ribbono shel 'Olam*, I know the outcome doesn't really matter, because it is all the same Being . . . It is all You, You, You, as Reb Levi Yitzhak of Berditchev says." But as we come back down from *Atzilut* and that 'You-ness,' we say, "But wouldn't it be nice if . . ." You almost want to tickle a willingness from God.

Question: Is there a place for those tightly held prayers? Actually, what I mean is, is there a place for pleading prayers, sometimes filled with deep sadness and desire?

Reb Zalman: Yes, of course. I remember a time around 1943 when my Rebbe was *davvenen* the *Amidah* on the first night of Rosh Hashanah, and the tears were pouring from him. We all had finished the *Amidah* already and he still hadn't gotten very far into it. So we were standing around reciting *T'hillim* while he cried through the *Amidah* for two hours!

Question: There is a sense of using various clever work-arounds in many of the prayer stories you have told; would you say that's an accurate description?

Reb Zalman: Yes, but not *merely* clever. They are clever with a deeply sincere and holy purpose; and more than that, they are pragmatic.

A long time ago I translated a story by Isaac Bashevis Singer called *"Yahid and Yehidah"* and sent it to him, saying, "If this is a story, I want to thank you for the wonderful story; but if the story is more than the story to you, I'd love to meet you." He writes back, "If you would like to meet me, and if the story is more than a story, then I want to meet you!" And so, when I came in from Manitoba, we went to the Famous Restaurant on 72nd Street, close to where he lived. He was a vegetarian, despite all the gross imagery in his writings. We had a wonderful conversation.

I was teaching Yiddish at that time and setting up a language lab, so I brought along a little tape recorder and he read me a wonderful story called, *"Di Ayitzeh."* The story was about a guy who is angry all the time and finds fault with everything, and generally leads an unhappy life. Finally, he comes to a Rebbe, Hazkele Kuzmirer, and asks the Rebbe for an *eitzah*, a 'prescription' for change. "What is it that you would suggest for me, because I'm eaten alive by this anger?"

The Rebbe says, "Become a flatterer."

Well, the man thought this was terrible and wanted to find fault with the Rebbe for suggesting it, but decided he had better try it. So he became a flatterer and everything shifted, because he couldn't just flatter people. He despised the whole idea of false flattery. So he had to find an actual good point in

Sixth Talk: The Rebbe's Tool-Box for Intercession

the people he flattered. And before long, his whole outlook on the world had changed!

Question: Do the possibilities and potentials seen by the Rebbe have an influence on the outcome?

Reb Zalman: This is a major emphasis in Hasidism.

A man comes to Reb Shalom Yosef, the Sadagerer Rebbe, and gives him a *kvittel*, a 'petitionary note.' He says Rebbe, "Would you please pray for" such and such an outcome.

The Rebbe says, "You better go to another Rebbe."

"Why?" he asks.

The Rebbe says, "Because I see that for the fulfillment of your *neshamah*, your 'soul,' what you are going through should not be lifted from you. If you insist, another Rebbe may see it differently."

Question: Very simply, could you just repeat the salient features of intercessory prayer again?

Reb Zalman: Of course:

1. I have the person in my mind, in my heart.
2. I take the 'elevator' up, as it were, into *Atzilut*, where both of us are 'chips off the old block,' and all is good. There is no evil there.
3. Then I descend into time and space and see the person in the full potential of their being in *B'riyah*. That's easy, because they're still in the 'womb of

their mother.'

4. Now comes the birth canal: *ḥesed, gevurah, tiferet, netzaḥ, hod*. This is where we really have to help out with the 'curling' mentioned earlier.

5. Then, in *yesod*, you 'save the file' you have been working on, the work you have done in that prayer and the outcome you hope to see. Action directives may also come in at this point.

6. Finally, I relinquish and let go of any expectations: "*Ribbono shel 'Olam*, it's now in your care."

Those are the steps.

Seventh Talk

A Dialogue on the Vocation of Being a Rebbe

Reb Netanel: Before we talk about anything else, I want to ask you—*What is a Rebbe?*

Reb Zalman: A Rebbe is a person whose soul also includes the souls of his or her Hasidim. When a Hasid comes to the Rebbe with a problem, the Rebbe attempts to locate and connect with the soul of that Hasid as a part of his or her own soul. And it is through the establishment of this connection that the Hasid receives material and spiritual benefit.

Reb Netanel: So a Rebbe has the capacity and skill to find the soul of another person *within*—a connection or resonance—and to offer a particular help based on an attunement to that resonance, one that is tailored to the Hasid's particular needs, yes?

Reb Zalman: Yes, but not always to the same degree. It can depend on how much intrinsic connection there is between the soul of the Rebbe and the particular Hasid. Rebbes have often sent potential Hasidim on in search of other guidance because there is a sense that the *shoresh ha'neshamah*, the 'root of that person's soul,' may not be, as it were, housed with that particular Rebbe. But if the Hasid belongs to the same *neshamah klalit,* 'general soul' or 'soul-cluster' as the Rebbe, then the guidance may come easier and with more clarity.

That is not to say that the Rebbe cannot function as a Rebbe for others 'outside of his or her network,' but that there may be more ambiguity or obstacles to overcome because the context is different.

Reb Netanel: Because not only is there a particular soul-affinity between a Rebbe and Hasid, being part of the same 'soul-cluster,' there is also a contract of intimacy between them, allowing for an unrestricted flow of information on different levels back and forth.

Reb Zalman: That's right. In the past, this was sometimes a formal contract, called a *k'tav hitkashrut,* a 'letter of self-binding' commitment to a Rebbe, such as several Hasidim gave the Malakh, the Maggid's only son after the Maggid of Mezritch's passing; but mostly it was understood. But whether written or not, the contract was clear.

Reb Netanel: A contract of intimacy and concern, and a contract to assist the Hasid in spiritual development?

Reb Zalman: Ideally. But, often, the people they were dealing with had more mundane concerns—children, the cows and the chickens. Some Rebbes did what they could for whomever came to them, with whatever need. Others, like the Kotzker Rebbe, forbade people to come to them with concerns about their cows! The ratio of spiritual to material concerns was

Seventh Talk: A Dialogue on the Vocation

perhaps best shown in a little anecdote about the Apter Rav, who got very excited when he got "a Ba'al Shemski *kvittel!*" That is to say, someone had brought him a prayer petition for a spiritual issue instead of the usual material prayer requests.

Of course, there were also Rebbes who saw themselves like kings looking after the material and spiritual welfare of their Hasidim. Nevertheless, the highest ideal in Hasidism was always to foster spiritual growth in Hasidim.

Reb Netanel: I find that I often have to explain the difference between a rabbi and Rebbe to people who don't have a sense of what Hasidism is, or that there are both normative and supra-normative approaches to Judaism. Given that we are talking about the Rebbe as a model of Jewish spiritual leadership here, perhaps you might clarify the differences?

Reb Zalman: A rabbi in the past was a legal authority, empowered by his learning and other authorities to make decisions on what was kosher and what was not. But today, the idea of the rabbi is more fluid. The rabbi of today also leads the prayer service, gives sermons, teaches classes and counsels members of his or her congregation. In this way, today's rabbi functions more like a Rebbe. But with an important distinction; the rabbi is still by-and-large a leader in an *external* sense, serving the Jewish needs of a community. The Rebbe, on the other hand, is working with the deeper, *internal* needs of people with whom he or she is in an intimate guidance relationship.

Reb Netanel: I think it is also worth saying that, while one might become a rabbi by education, by studying in a *yeshiva* or going through an ordination program, one does not become a Rebbe in the same way. While rabbis may be more or less skillful or talented and have the same basic ordination, having demonstrated a certain mastery of information, a Rebbe's mastery is not a mastery of *information,* but of *attunement.*

Reb Zalman: The Rebbe's attunement is crucial. When I look at the original story of how the Ba'al Shem Tov challenged the Maggid of Mezritch to read and offer an explanation of a passage in the Luria's *Eitz Hayyim,* I ask, "Why did the Maggid fail?" He offered a good explanation; it was all correct, a good head answer. In that, he was a good rabbi and good kabbalist in the knowledge sense. But he was not yet attuned to the reality beneath the words.

All the Ba'al Shem Tov had to do was read and give over the same passage with attunement and the Maggid felt the reality beneath the words and became his disciple in order to learn how to do that himself. And he got it, and for several generations, he and his students were able to transmit that attunement to others. But attunement is not verbal, it's not left brain, so there is no way to write about that or get it through reading alone.

No, not everyone can become a Rebbe, and certainly not by education; one needs something from *Above* to fullfil this mission.

Reb Netanel: Throughout these talks, you have openly discussed the role and function of a Rebbe as a model of spiritual leadership, and I agree that it is necessary to do so; but I also feel the message might be misunderstood and play into our usual Western cultural dysfunction, seeing Rebbe-hood as just another opportunity for the ego to shine, as a

Seventh Talk: A Dialogue on the Vocation

goal at the peak of Jewish spirituality. But Rebbe-hood is so clearly not the goal, at least not in Hasidism. *The goal is to become a Hasid,* even for the Rebbe.

In my eyes, Rebbe-hood is a vocation, a role and a function to be fulfilled by those who are called to it, by those who cannot avoid it; but not a goal in itself. If anything, the Rebbe is modeling how to be *Hasid,* with an open vertical connection, in a continuing relationship with his or her own Rebbe, and especially with God.

Reb Zalman: That's right. The Rebbe is still participating in a continuum of abasement like the Hasid, abasing the ego before *their own* Rebbe (who may even have passed on), and most importantly, the Blessed and Holy One. The Rebbe is fulfilling—what I would call today—a *temporary* vocational function for others; but is still, according to the ideal, intending only to be a Hasid.

This is what I was saying earlier about the Rebbe being a symbol and a facilitator for the soul-cluster. Take a light bulb as an example. The bulb itself cannot give off any light; it is simply a vehicle for the light. The electricity and light bulb source are actually from a power plant in some distant part of the city. But there must also be some resemblance in the bulb which enables it to receive power from the source—a wire, a contact—which connects it to the power source. Then, with the flip of a switch, the flow of electricity is opened, allowing the bulb to receive power and to function as a light bulb.

In the same way, the Rebbe is not the Light, but its servant, receiving energy from God, the Power Source. And it is only by his or her own effacement and transparency that the Light shines through. The Rebbe's real contribution to the process is in *serving* as a conduit—and here the metaphor breaks down a bit—in consciously recognizing the internal similarities and connections, and in knowing how to flip the switch.

Reb Netanel: Back when I used to assist you in teaching a class you called, "Issues in Spiritual Direction," for people who were studying to be clergy and transpersonal therapists at Naropa University, I noticed the same basic problem. There was a clear desire among many of them *to be and see themselves* as spiritual leaders, when many of them had never been led, never known what it was to be a disciple.

If someone has never been a disciple, it seems to me, there is a good possibility that they may not have the proper respect for a disciple.

Reb Zalman: When somebody wants to be a Rebbe, without having served as a Hasid, it won't work. What makes a Rebbe *real* is having spent time in the discipline of being a true disciple, of being a Hasid. The ego-reduction that has to happen to prepare someone for deep study, effective prayer, and for handling the responsibilities of *yehidut*, comes through conscious abasement to the preceptor, the Rebbe, for the purpose of learning the Rebbe's *attunement*.

Take the example of Reb Mordecai Yosef of Ishbitz, a great Rebbe who had been a devoted Hasid. When he first came to Reb Simhah Bunim as a young man, he was not as tall as Reb Simhah Bunim. So Reb Simhah Bunim says, "Come, let's measure ourselves back-to-back." And when they had, he said, "Now I am taller than you; but you'll grow, and there will come a time when you are taller than I."

Reb Mordecai Yosef was a complete disciple to Reb

Seventh Talk: A Dialogue on the Vocation

Simhah Bunim. And later, he also submitted himself for an additional 13 years to the Kotzker Rebbe, who had been the senior disciple of Reb Simhah Bunim. Toward the end of that time, the Kotzker Rebbe secluded himself more and more and gave over more responsibilities to Reb Mordecai Yosef. Indeed, he had put him in charge of the younger Hasidim. So, one day, when Reb Mordecai Yosef was about to depart from Kotzk, he went to give his regards to the Kotzker's son, Reb Dovid. Reb Dovid says to him, "Go in peace; but where is the *letzgelt,* some goodbye money." Like paying your dues to the organization. So Reb Mordecai Yosef reaches into his pocket to take out some money, but when he pulls his hands out of his pockets, some *kvittlakh,* 'petitionary notes' from the Hasidim fall out on the ground. Reb Dovid, who sees this as a threat to his father's leadership says, *"Ah-h-h!* So you're taking *kvittlakh* already!" Reb Mordecai Yosef leans down, picks up the *kvittlakh,* stands and looks at Reb Dovid in the eye and says, "What do you think I came to learn from your father, to be a shoemaker?"

Reb Netanel: Reb Mordecai Yosef, the Ishbitzer, knows he has a vocation as a Rebbe, and he knows because the people come to him.

Reb Zalman: And also because Reb Mendel, the Kotzker, had already entrusted him with responsibility for the younger Hasidim. Why else would he do that?

Reb Netanel: So the knowledge of the vocation comes both ways to him, from below and above. And when it is clear, he takes responsibility for learning how to do that well.

Reb Zalman: That's the point of how to become a Rebbe: *you watch and observe.* It's the same situation we see with Reb Ahrele Roth and the Bluzhover Rebbe. The Bluzhover Rebbe says to his Hasidim, "You are all nice Hasidim, but this Hungarian boy watches everything I do to see what *yihud* I am making!"

Reb Menachem Mendel, who became the seventh Lubavitcher Rebbe, kept journals in which he recorded what he saw and learned from Reb Yosef Yitzhak, the sixth Lubavitcher Rebbe. He was paying attention and watched with the right kind of eye.

At the same time, there are some people who, even if they don't have the vocation, are resting too much in the idea of being a Hasid, being a follower, and not really looking at how to make changes in their lives, not taking responsibility for their own situations. They like to hear and be near the Rebbe, but not to watch close for how to make changes. That was what we saw with many Hasidic lineages who interpreted "The *tzaddik* lives by faith" (Hab. 2:4) as "The *tzaddik* gives life with his faith." So all the special spiritual work is for the Rebbe alone, and not for the Hasid. The Rebbe does it for you. And that's an attitude we can't afford.

Reb Netanel: So this is the way in which the Rebbe is a model for spiritual leadership; in modeling how to be a Hasid while in a leadership position, the Rebbe provides an example of real service and humility, as well as a living frequency to which Hasidim and leaders of all types might attune themselves.

Reb Zalman: That "living frequency" is what is most important. You can tell someone how to do things, you can write a book about reading a *kvittel* or other shamanic things, but it's only words. You have to attune to a person who is actually doing it to really know what it is about.

Reb Netanel: A kind of intimate apprenticeship is necessary, where one learns both the external and internal qualities of how it is done by observation and feedback.

Reb Zalman: A person doesn't become a Rebbe overnight, or without some checks. When my Rebbe, Reb Yosef Yitzhak, was a young man, his father, the fifth Lubavitcher Rebbe put him in charge of the *yeshiva,* and put him into a counseling position with the students. He would work with them and then bring both their issues and what he had recommended back to his father for refinement. It was a supervised process for him.

For years, I did this with the Rebbe, Reb Menachem Mendel, in *yeḥidut,* and through the letters I sent to him about what I was doing, and what I was recommending. And he would write back refinements and corrections. That feedback was critical to my development.

But I also want to say that there is lateral feedback that is also important. And this comes back to the issue of having been a Hasid before becoming a Rebbe. If a person becomes a Rebbe without having first been a Hasid *among Hasidim*—which has happened—there is something missing in their leadership.

Reb Netanel: You mean, without having experienced that fellowship, the common concerns, and the checks that come from spiritual friends?

Reb Zalman: It's important to have buddies, like Reb Dov

Baer of Lubavitch said about having a spiritual companion: "That way, you have two *yetzer ha'tov*'s against one *yetzer ha'ra.*" Spiritual loners who have not come out of this kind of context, and yet who have become leaders, often don't have a respect for feedback.

Responsibility—*answerability*—is very important. I have seen talented, self-made people in Rebbe-positions who didn't feel they were answerable to anyone, who thought that they were smarter and knew more than everyone, and so never checked anything out with anyone else. And I have seen others of this sort who were very, very good, but who had no feedback opening, and so would often talk and talk without reading the needs of the group. In this situation, the connection is lost, but they just continue talking.

It so important to have a spiritual friend, or friends, to give you feedback, to laugh with and keep you from taking yourself too seriously. You don't get teased if you just become a Rebbe without having been a Hasid.

Reb Netanel: We see that your Rebbe, Reb Yosef Yitzhak, was *among* the Hasidim throughout his youth.

Reb Zalman: As a child, the older Hasidim were always around and they liked him.

Reb Netanel: And he talked to them and listened to their stories, and sat among them watching his father, a Hasid among Hasidim.

Reb Zalman: And that showed itself in the way he related

Seventh Talk: A Dialogue on the Vocation

to Hasidim later when he was a Rebbe. In his talks, as was the case in his father's time, there would be dialogue with the Hasidim; it wasn't just a one-way thing. He was really listening to them and their concerns.

Did you get to see the documentary, *Kumaré*, about the young Indian-American filmmaker who fakes an Indian accent and pretends to be an authentic *guru* in Arizona?

Reb Netanel: I did. It was amazing—both in its illustration of our cultural dysfunctionality around spirituality, and in the authentic teachings that managed to come through.

Reb Zalman: You saw how things changed? How he switched from mockery because he found himself actually listening to the people who came to him?

Reb Netanel: Yes, and you could see exactly when the switch occurred: the moment he felt the weight of what was being brought to him—the heavy things people were dealing with—and how they expected answers from him that would actually work. Then he began to understand what a responsibility it is to be a spiritual leader. No one who doesn't listen, and who doesn't feel that burden should be offering advice.

Reb Zalman: Another thing I want to say about being a Hasid among Hasidim is about the training that happens there with mentors. As much contact as I had with the sixth and seventh Rebbes of Lubavitch, I had more with my *mashpiyyim*, with my 'mentors' who were senior Hasidim of the Rebbe, especially in my youth. These were venerable Hasidim like Reb Yisroel

Jacobson, Reb Eliya Simpson, Reb Shmuel Levitin, and Reb Avraham Pariz.

We need to emphasize these relationships in our situation as well. We need more *mashpiyyim* who are good adepts and guides to mentor others, and more people to actively seek them out. It can't all depend on a single person, on a Rebbe, who is supposed to do everything. The Rebbe needs a lot of support staff.

Remember the story about the Ba'al Shem Tov and the ladder?

Reb Netanel: When the Ba'al Shem Tov was praying and saw himself as climbing a scaffold of Hasidim to reach the golden bird in the top of the tree?

Reb Zalman: And just as he is about to reach it, the scaffold collapses! While he was praying, the Hasidim had gotten tired and had gone home. You see, he couldn't do it without them, and they didn't understand their role in the work that was being done.

When I was leading retreats at Fellowship House and Farm in Pennsylvania, so often I had to be both the Rebbe and the *shammes,* putting out chairs, distributing papers and arranging everything. No one was supporting me; and yet, people came up to me while I was doing these things and expected me to function like a Rebbe for them! How could I be in that mindspace when I had to do these things? You cannot function as the Rebbe when you are setting up the tables and chairs. If someone wants *yehidut,* I would say, "Let me prepare and get into that place first."

Seventh Talk: A Dialogue on the Vocation

Look, if I had to do all that you and others are doing for me at this point in my life, I would never even get a chance to say, "Hello, God." For a Rebbe to function, there needs to be three or four people supporting them in that work.

Reb Netanel: That's a good way of looking at the whole situation: there is no Rebbe without Hasidim; and without the people supporting the Rebbe-function, *there is no Rebbe-function at all.*

Reb Zalman: And we need that function, and the wisdom of how to do it, to continue to help us map our future.

Do you remember the story of Reb Elimelekh of Lizhensk and the Seer of Lublin, about the Rebbe's 'event horizon'? It shows us that there is some overlap necessary, disciples who can take up the reins in the Rebbe's lifetime, because there are things coming up that impact the next generation that the Rebbe before doesn't handle; they may contribute a piece to it, but it is not entirely theirs to take on. So the work must be continued by the Rebbes that follow.

Appendix

Training the Rebbes of the Future

IN THESE TUMULTUOUS TIMES, people have a very great need for genuine healers of the spirit. Many Rebbes will have to be trained to provide meaningful counsel. Yet, within virtually every form of spiritual training, certain aspects are more essential than others. So too with Hasidism. What then are the key characteristics one must acquire to be a true Rebbe?

The following seven traits seem most crucial to us:

1. An experience of kinship with other beings on the planet—that is, a sense of compassion transcending the bounds of ego, time and place.
2. An inner awakening, in which one encounters the realm of the transcendent, however fleeting or incomplete that sacred moment may be.
3. A thorough understanding—and working-through—of one's own emotional imbalances. In this way, one will be less likely to project his or her problems onto those seeking advice.
4. A firm grounding in one's own body awareness, so that one is comfortable—neither anxious nor obsessed—about dealing with the sensual world.
5. A comprehensive philosophical-intellectual training, enabling one to grasp a variety of reality-

maps of consciousness, not just the everyday reality of human existence.

6. A well-developed sense of intuition, so that one knows when to discard rote principles and generalizations and rely instead on personal hunches.

7. An active participation in a community or network, so that one can engage in honest soul-searching with others as friendly critics and guides.[13]

---

[13] First formulated for inclusion in Zalman M. Schachter and Edward Hoffman, *Sparks of Light: Counseling in the Hasidic Tradition* (1983), 186-87.

The Geologists of the Soul Forum

www.geologistsofthesoul.com

Moderated by
Amitai Zachary Malone

THE GEOLOGISTS OF THE SOUL FORUM is inspired by the life and teachings of Rabbi Zalman Schachter-Shalomi, and is intended to be a forum for today's 'Geologists of the Soul,' the most inspired teachers and spiritual mentors of the Abrahamic traditions whom we are lucky enough to have access to at this time in the world.

In this forum, we hope to present a series of interviews with these teachers which will become the basis for an ongoing dialogue addressing critical issues in the spiritual life, especially as it is unfolding in the 21st century.

It is our hope that this site will be a help and support to all of those who are dedicated to finding the inner treasure of Divinity.

— *Amitai Zachary Malone, Boulder, Colorado*

www.ingramcontent.com/pod-product-compliance
Lightning Source LLC
Chambersburg PA
CBHW022110090426
42743CB00008B/798